In Th[is...]

QuickSta[rt] Guide

Your keys to understanding the city – we help you decide what to do and how to do it

N...
Tips ...
smooth...

Local ...

The inside...

Top Sights

Make the most of your visit

Edinburgh's Best...

The best experiences

Explore Edinburgh

The best things to see and do, neighbourhood by neighbourhood

Best Walks

See the city on foot

Essential Information

Including where to st[ay]

The Best of Edinburgh

The city's highlights in handy lists to help you plan

Getting Around

Travel like a local

Survival Guide

Tips and tricks for a seamless, hassle-free city experience

Our selection of the city's best places to eat, drink and experience:

- ◎ **Sights**
- ✖ **Eating**
- 🍷 **Drinking**
- ✦ **Entertainment**
- 🔒 **Shopping**

These symbols give you the vital information for each listing:

- 🎵 Telephone Numbers
- ⊙ Opening Hours
- P Parking
- ⊖ Nonsmoking
- @ Internet Access
- 🛜 Wi-Fi Access
- 🌱 Vegetarian Selection
- 👪 Family-Friendly
- 🐾 Pet-Friendly
- 🚌 Bus
- ⛴ Ferry
- Ⓜ Metro
- Ⓢ Subway
- 🚊 Tram
- 🚆 Train

Find each listing quickly on maps for each neighbourhood:

Bar Hemingway

16 📍 Map p233, B2

Legend has it that Hemi self, wielding a machine rate this timber-pan ered bar during showpiece is a en by Papa an town. Dress s.com; Hôtel Rit ⊙6.30pm-2a

6 ◎ Plac

Lonely ...
Edinburg...

Lonely Planet ...
are designed to g...
straight to the hear...

Inside you'll find al...
must-see sights, plus ti...
make your visit to each or
really memorable. We've sp...
the city into easy-to-navigate
neighbourhoods and provided
clear maps so you'll find your
way around with ease. Our
expert authors have searched
out the best of the city: walks,
food, nightlife and shopping,
to name a few. Because you
want to explore, our 'Local Life'
pages will take you to some
of the most exciting areas to
experience the real Edinburgh.

And of course you'll find all
the practical tips you need for
a smooth trip: itineraries for
short visits, how to get around,
and how much to tip the guy
who serves you a drink at the
end of a long day's exploration.
It's your guarantee of a
really great experience.

Our Promise

You can trust our travel information because Lonely Planet
authors visit the places we
write about, each and every
edition. We never accept
freebies for positive coverage,
so you can rely on us to tell it
like it is.

Explore Edinburgh 21

The Best of Edinburgh 133

Edinburgh's Best Walks

Edinburgh's Best ...

Survival Guide 153

QuickStart Guide

Welcome to Edinburgh

Edinburgh is one of Britain's most beautiful cities, 'a dream in masonry and living rock' perched upon ancient crags, with the medieval maze of the Old Town gazing across verdant gardens to the Georgian elegance of the New Town. History and architecture are leavened with a bacchanalia of bars, innovative restaurants and Scotland's most stylish shops, all wrapped in a cityscape immortalised in literature and film.

View over Edinburgh from Calton Hill (p77)
CHRIS HEPBURN/GETTY IMAGES ©

Edinburgh Top Sights

Edinburgh Castle (p24)

Attracting more than 1.3 million visitors a year, Edinburgh Castle is Scotland's most popular attraction, a craggy cluster of museums, militaria, chapels, cannons, vaults and prisons, and the Scottish Crown Jewels.

MARK A. JOHNSON/CORBIS ©

Rosslyn Chapel (p130)

Made famous by Dan Brown's *The Da Vinci Code*, this medieval chapel is a symphony in stone, thickly clustered with carved symbols and imagery that has been associated with the enigmatic quest for the Holy Grail.

Royal Yacht Britannia (p112)

Since her retirement in 1997, the former floating holiday home of the British royal family has been moored at Leith's Ocean Terminal, offering a fascinating insight into HM the Queen's travels.

Real Mary King's Close
(p28)

Sealed off in the 18th century, this buried medieval street was opened to the public in 2003, offering atmospheric guided tours of its ancient vaults.

Scottish Parliament Building (p58)

Edinburgh's most spectacular and controversial building, opened in 2004 to house Scotland's devolved parliament, is a confection of strange shapes and symbolic forms.

Palace of Holyroodhouse
(p56)

The queen's official residence in Scotland has at its heart a tower house that was once home to Mary, Queen of Scots: her bedchamber is the high point of the tour.

National Museum of Scotland (p30)

This museum charts the history of Scotland. Highlights include the Monymusk Reliquary, carried into battle at Bannockburn, and the 12th-century Lewis Chessmen.

Scottish National Portrait Gallery (p68)

This beautifully renovated gallery is now one of the city's top sights, leading visitors entertainingly through Scottish history by means of portraits of famous characters.

Princes Street Gardens (p70)

One of Britain's most dramatically situated city parks, this garden lines a verdant valley between the spire-spiked skyline of the Old Town and ordered elegance of the New Town.

VISITBRITAIN/BRITAIN ON VIEW/GETTY IMAGES ©

VISITBRITAIN/BRITAIN ON VIEW/GETTY IMAGES ©

KARL BLACKWELL/GETTY IMAGES ©

KARL BLACKWELL/GETTY IMAGES ©

Scottish National Gallery of Modern Art (p92)

Devoted to 20th-century and contemporary art, this gallery is housed in two impressive neo-classical buildings set in gorgeous grounds dotted with sculptures.

Royal Botanic Garden (p102)

These 70 landscaped acres include splendid Victorian glasshouses, giant Amazonian water lilies, colourful swathes of rhododendron and azalea, and a famous rock garden.

Edinburgh Local Life

Insider tips to help you find the real city

There's more to Edinburgh than the top tourist sights. Experience a little of what makes the city tick by exploring its hidden backstreets, stylish shops, scenic parkland, and a village within the city.

Explore the Old Town's Hidden History (p34)

▶ Hidden alleys
▶ Historic sites

Much of what makes Edinburgh's Old Town so intriguing is its maze of narrow wynds (alleys) and staircases connecting different levels of the city. Most visitors don't stray from the Royal Mile, but to really appreciate Old Town history you have to delve into the network of hidden alleyways.

A Walk Through Holyrood Park (p60)

▶ City-centre scenery
▶ Panoramic views

Holyrood Park, the former hunting ground of Scottish kings, brings a huge chunk of countryside into the heart of the city. Put on your hiking shoes and explore the walking trails that criss-cross its slopes, leading eventually to the picturesque village of Duddingston and its welcoming country pub.

New Town Shopping (p72)

▶ Georgian architecture
▶ Upmarket shops

Once the powerhouse of Edinburgh's financial industry, the New Town's smart Georgian streets have been taken over by a wealth of classy shops and designer outlets. Grab your credit cards and search for that something special in the gorgeous boutiques on Thistle St, before relaxing in one of the city's top lunch spots.

A Sunday Stroll Around Stockbridge (p104)

▶ Unique shops
▶ Stylish street life

Stockbridge began life as a mill village on the Water of Leith, but has long since been swept up in Edinburgh's urban expansion. Enjoy a stroll around one of the city's most desirable districts, home to offbeat boutiques, cute cafes, great neighbourhood bistros and Scotland's best Sunday market.

Georgian architecture of the New Town (p66)

Boathouse on the Union Canal (p124)

Other great places to experience the city like a local:

Cockburn Street Shops (p52)

Edinburgh's Mysterious Book Sculptures (p42)

Sandy Bell's (p50)

Urban Hillwalking on Arthur's Seat (p65)

Edinburgh Farmers Market (p96)

Bohemian Broughton (p83)

Cramond Village (p116)

Union Canal (p124)

Southside Brunch (p126)

Edinburgh Zoo (p85)

Edinburgh Day Planner

Day One

Edinburgh Castle (p24) is the city's number one sight, so if you only have a day to spare, spend at least the first two hours after opening time here. Take a leisurely stroll down the Royal Mile, stopping off for a pre-booked tour of the historic Real Mary King's Close (p28) before having lunch at Wedgwood (p44) or Foodies (p64).

At the bottom of the Mile, take a one-hour guided tour of the Scottish Parliament Building (p58), before crossing the street to the Palace of Holyroodhouse (p56). Then, if the weather's fine, take an early-evening stroll along Radical Road at the foot of Salisbury Crags, or head up the stairs from nearby Calton Rd to the summit of Calton Hill (p77); both offer superb views across the city.

Round off the day with dinner at a restaurant with a view such as the Tower (p45). If the weather's not so hot, try somewhere more cosy and romantic, like Witchery by the Castle (p45) or Ondine (p44). Either pre- or post-dinner, try to catch a play at the Traverse Theatre (p99) or scare yourself silly on a ghost tour of Greyfriars Kirkyard (p35).

Day Two

Make morning number two a feast of culture, with a tour of the recently revamped exhibits in the National Museum of Scotland (p30), followed by a short stroll down the Mound – with great views across Princes Street Gardens and the New Town – to the iconic artworks of the Scottish National Gallery (p76).

Try a lunch of haggis or Cullen skink in the gallery's Scottish Cafe & Restaurant (p71), then work off those calories by climbing to the top of the nearby Scott Monument (p71) for even better views. Catch a bus on Princes St and relax as you head to Ocean Terminal for a visit to the Royal Yacht Britannia (p112).

Time your trip to get the last two hours of opening at Britannia, then head for a pre-booked dinner at one of Leith's many fine restaurants – Martin Wishart (p116) for fine French dining, or Fishers Bistro (p116) for fresh seafood. Stay in Leith for a pint at Teuchters Landing (p118) or a cocktail in a teapot at the Roseleaf (p117), or head back to the city centre to sample some Edinburgh-brewed beer in the magnificent surroundings of the Café Royal Circle Bar (p84).

Short on time?
We've arranged Edinburgh's must-sees into these day-by-day itineraries to make sure you see the very best of the city in the time you have available.

Day Three

Fingers crossed and hope for good weather – begin the day with a visit to the **Scottish National Gallery of Modern Art** (p92), then enjoy a surprisingly bucolic walk along the Water of Leith Walkway to **Stockbridge** where you can explore the boutiques on **St Stephen Street** before pausing for a refreshing pint in the **Stockbridge Tap** (p108).

If it's Sunday, spend an hour or so browsing the stalls at **Stockbridge Market**, then make the short stroll to the **Royal Botanic Garden** (p102). If you didn't have lunch in Stockbridge, head to the garden's Gateway Restaurant or Terrace Cafe. This is one of the UK's leading botanic gardens, so devote the rest of the afternoon to exploring the palm houses, rock gardens, woodland gardens and outdoor sculptures.

In the evening, treat yourself to a decadent dinner amid the Gothic grandeur of **Rhubarb** (p64) or the Georgian elegance of **21212** (p83). Have tickets booked for a show at the **Lyceum** (p99) or the **Playhouse** (p87), or head for late-night cocktails at **Bramble** (p84) or **Lulu** (p86).

Day Four

Devote an entire morning to the Da Vinci Code delights of **Rosslyn Chapel** (p131), on the southern fringes of the city. This 15th-century church is a monument to the stonemason's art, and so crammed with arcane symbolism that it has inspired countless conspiracy theories about possible links to the Knights Templar and the quest for the Holy Grail. Have lunch at the chapel's coffee shop.

Return to the city centre to spend the afternoon browsing the boutiques and department stores of the **New Town**, while soaking up the atmosphere of the world's best-preserved Georgian townscape. Take an hour or so to wander around the **Scottish National Portrait Gallery** (p68), which leads you entertainingly through Scottish history via portraits of famous personalities.

Take an early-evening stroll through **Princes Street Gardens** (p70) then wander down Leith Walk to **Joseph Pearce's** (p84) for a gin and tonic before tucking into a tasty organic dinner at the delightful **Gardener's Cottage** (p81); book ahead. Round off the evening with some live jazz at the **Jam House** (p86), or a comedy act at **The Stand** (p86).

Need to Know

For more information, see Survival Guide (p153)

Currency
Pound sterling (£). 100 pence = £1

Language
English

Visas
Generally not needed for stays of up to six months. Not a member of the Schengen Zone.

Money
ATMs widespread. Major credit cards accepted everywhere.

Mobile Phones
Uses the GSM 900/1800 network. Local SIM cards can be used in European and Australian phones.

Time
Edinburgh is on GMT; during British Summer Time (BST; last Sunday in March to last Saturday in October) clocks are one hour ahead of GMT.

Plugs & Adaptors
Standard voltage is 230-240V AC, 50 Hz. Three square-pin plugs. Adaptors for European, Australasian and American electrical items are widely available.

Tipping
Tip restaurant waiting staff 10% to 15% unless service is included. Locals generally don't tip taxi drivers.

 **Before You Go**

Your Daily Budget

Budget less than £50
▶ Dorm beds £15–30
▶ Markets and lunch specials for food
▶ Loads of free museums and galleries

Midrange £50–120
▶ Double room £80–100
▶ Two-course dinner with glass of wine £30
▶ Live music in pub free–£10

Top End over £120
▶ Double room in boutique or four-star hotel £175–225
▶ Three-course dinner in top restaurant including wine £70–100
▶ Taxi across town £15

Useful Websites

Lonely Planet (www.lonelyplanet.com/edinburgh) Destination info, hotel bookings, great for planning.

VisitScotland Edinburgh (www.edinburgh.org) Official Scottish tourist board site.

The List (www.list.co.uk) Listings and reviews for restaurants, bars, clubs and theatres.

Advance Planning

Six months Book accommodation for August festival period. Book a table at the Witchery by the Castle restaurant.

Two months Book accommodation; reserve tables in top restaurants; book car hire.

One month Buy tickets online for Edinburgh Castle and Rosslyn Chapel; check listings for entertainment and book tickets.

② Arriving in Edinburgh

Most visitors arrive at Edinburgh Airport (www.edinburghairport.com), 8 miles west of the city centre, or at Edinburgh Waverley train station, right in the heart of the city between the Old Town and New Town.

From 2014 a brand-new tram line (www.edinburghtrams.com) will be running from Edinburgh Airport to the city centre.

✈ Edinburgh Airport

Destination	Best Transport
Old Town	Airlink Bus 100
New Town	Airlink Bus 100
West End	Airlink Bus 100
South Edinburgh	Airlink Bus 100, then connecting bus or taxi
Leith	Airlink Bus 100, then connecting bus or taxi

🚌 From Edinburgh Waverley Train Station

Taxi rank in station. Short walk to Princes St, where buses depart to all parts of the city.

✈ At the Airport

The arrivals hall has a tourist information and accommodation desk, left-luggage facilities, ATMs, currency exchange desks, shops, restaurants, internet access and car-hire agencies. Turn left out of arrivals to find the Airlink Bus 100 stop, and the taxi ranks.

③ Getting Around

Up to 2014, public transport within the city was provided entirely by buses; the two main operators are Lothian Buses (www.lothianbuses.com), which runs most of the city routes, and First Edinburgh (www.first edinburgh.co.uk), with buses mainly serving the towns and villages around Edinburgh. From 2014 a brand-new tram line (www.edinburghtrams.com) will be running from Edinburgh Airport to the city centre.

🚌 Bus

The bus network is extensive and is the best way of getting from the suburbs to the centre, and for north–south trips. Despite dedicated bus lanes, buses can get held up in traffic during rush hours.

🚋 Tram

Fast and frequent (every 10 to 12 minutes) service from the airport to York Place in the east of the city centre, via Murrayfield Stadium, Haymarket, the West End and Princes St.

🚕 Taxi

Friendly and knowledgeable drivers, great for late-night journeys, but fares can be expensive unless there are four people sharing.

🚲 Bicycle

Great for leisure – hire a bike and escape to the countryside via the Water of Leith Walkway, or the Union Canal towpath.

🚗 Car & Motorcycle

As a visitor, it's unlikely you'll need to drive. Disincentives include the difficulty of finding a parking place, high parking charges, and traffic congestion, especially during rush hours.

Edinburgh Neighbourhoods

New Town (p66)

Georgian terraces lined with designer boutiques, wine bars and cocktail lounges, plus Princes Street Gardens and the perfect viewpoint of Calton Hill.

◉ Top Sights

Scottish National Portrait Gallery

Princes Street Gardens

Stockbridge (p100)

A former village with its own distinct identity, stylish and quirky shops and a good choice of pubs and restaurants.

◉ Top Sights

Royal Botanic Garden

West End & Dean Village (p90)

More Georgian elegance and upmarket shops, leading down to the picturesque Dean Village in the wooded valley of the Water of Leith.

◉ Top Sights

Scottish National Gallery of Modern Art

South Edinburgh (p120)

A peaceful residential area of Victorian tenement flats and spacious garden villas; not much in the way of tourist attractions, but good walking territory and many good restaurants and pubs.

◉ Royal Botanic Garden

◉ Scottish National Gallery of Modern Art

Princes Street Gardens ◉

Edinburgh Castle ◉

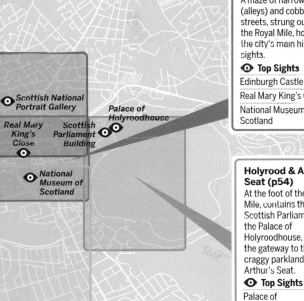

Royal Yacht Britannia

Leith (p110)
Redeveloped industrial docklands now occupied by restaurants, bars and Ocean Terminal, the city's biggest shopping centre.

⊙ Top Sights

Royal Yacht Britannia

Old Town (p22)
A maze of narrow wynds (alleys) and cobbled streets, strung out along the Royal Mile, home to the city's main historical sights.

⊙ Top Sights

Edinburgh Castle

Real Mary King's Close

National Museum of Scotland

Scottish National Portrait Gallery

Real Mary King's Close

Scottish Parliament Building

Palace of Holyroodhouse

National Museum of Scotland

Holyrood & Arthur's Seat (p54)
At the foot of the Royal Mile, contains the Scottish Parliament and the Palace of Holyroodhouse, and is the gateway to the craggy parkland of Arthur's Seat.

⊙ Top Sights

Palace of Holyroodhouse

Scottish Parliament Building

Worth a Trip

⊙ Top Sights

Rosslyn Chapel

Explore
Edinburgh

Morning in Edinburgh, viewed from Arthur's Seat (p63)
JOHN AND TINA REID/GETTY IMAGES ©

Explore

Old Town

Edinburgh's Old Town is a jagged, jumbled maze of historic masonry riddled with closes, stairs, vaults and wynds (narrow alleys) leading off the cobbled ravine of the Royal Mile, which links Edinburgh Castle to the Palace of Holyroodhouse. The restored 16th- and 17th-century Old Town tenements support a thriving city-centre community, crammed at street level with museums, restaurants, bars and shops.

The Sights in a Day

☀ Be at **Edinburgh Castle** (p24) for opening time, and plan on spending two hours exploring its many attractions before heading downhill along the Royal Mile, stopping off as the fancy takes you at the **Scotch Whisky Experience** (p40), the **Camera Obscura** (p43) and **Gladstone's Land** (p41).

☀ Continue down the Royal Mile, taking a quick look at **St Giles Cathedral** (p38) and **John Knox House** (p42) before taking a tour of either **Real Mary King's Close** (p28) or the **National Museum of Scotland** (p30). Get your photo taken beside the statue of **Greyfriars Bobby** (p42) and then take a stroll around Greyfriars Kirkyard, before heading down to the Grassmarket for a drink, and a look at the shops in atmospheric Victoria St (pictured left).

☾ Book a late dinner at either **Ondine** (p44), **Witchery by the Castle** (p45) or **Wedgwood** (p44), and join a **ghost tour** (p46) of Greyfriars Kirkyard to work up an appetite. Or dine around 7pm then head to **Sandy Bell's** (p50) for some live Scottish folk music.

For a local's day in the Old Town, see p34.

⊙ Top Sights

Edinburgh Castle (p24)

Real Mary King's Close (p28)

National Museum of Scotland (p30)

◯ Local Life

Explore the Old Town's Hidden History (p34)

♥ Best of Edinburgh

Eating

Ondine (p44)

Wedgwood (p44)

Tower (p45)

David Bann (p45)

Witchery by the Castle (p45)

Amber (p45)

Museums & Galleries

National Museum of Scotland (p30)

Museum of Edinburgh (p40)

Getting There

🚌 **Bus** Lothian Buses No 35 runs along the lower part of the Royal Mile from George IV Bridge to the Palace of Holyroodhouse; No 36 links Princes St to the Scottish Parliament via St Mary's St and Holyrood Rd. Buses 23, 27, 41 and 42 run along the Mound and George IV Bridge, giving access to the Royal Mile and Grassmarket (via Victoria St or Candlemaker Row).

Top Sights
Edinburgh Castle

The brooding black crags of Castle Rock, rising above the western end of Princes St, are the very reason for Edinburgh's existence. This rocky hill was the most easily defended hilltop on the invasion route between England and central Scotland. The castle last saw military action in 1745; from then until the 1920s it served as the British army's main base in Scotland. Today it is one of Scotland's most atmospheric and popular tourist attractions.

👁 Map p36, A3

www.edinburghcastle.gov.uk

adult/child incl audioguide £16/9.60

🕘 9.30am-6pm Apr-Sep, to 5pm Oct-Mar

🚌 23, 27, 41 or 42

Don't Miss

The Esplanade

The castle's **Esplanade** is a parade ground dating from 1820, with superb views south over the city towards the Pentland Hills. At its western end is the **Entrance Gateway**, dating from 1888 and flanked by statues of Robert the Bruce and William Wallace. Above the gate is the Royal Standard of Scotland – a red lion rampant on a gold field – and the Scottish Royal motto in Latin, 'Nemo me impune lacessit.' This translates into Scots as 'wha daur meddle wi' me', and into English as 'watch it, pal' (OK, it literally means 'no one provokes me with impunity').

One O'Clock Gun

Inside the entrance, a cobbled lane leads up beneath the 16th-century **Portcullis Gate**, topped by the 19th-century Argyle Tower, and past the cannon of the Argyle and Mills Mount Batteries. The battlements here have great views over the New Town to the Firth of Forth. At the far end of Mills Mount Battery is the **One O'Clock Gun**, a gleaming WWII 25-pounder that fires an ear-splitting time signal at 1pm every day (except Sundays, Christmas Day and Good Friday).

St Margaret's Chapel

South of Mills Mount, the road curls up leftwards through **Foog's Gate** to the highest part of Castle Rock, crowned by the tiny **St Margaret's Chapel**, the oldest surviving building in Edinburgh. It's a simple Romanesque structure that was probably built by David I or Alexander I in memory of their mother Queen Margaret sometime around 1130 (she was canonised in 1250). Following Cromwell's capture of the castle in 1650 it was used to store ammunition until it was restored

☑ Top Tips

▶ If you're pushed for time, the top five things to see at Edinburgh Castle are: views from the Argyle Battery; the One O'Clock Gun; the Great Hall; the Honours of Scotland; and the Prisons of War exhibition.

▶ Avoid ticket-office queues by purchasing your tickets online via the Edinburgh Castle website.

▶ Time your visit to coincide with the firing of the One O'Clock Gun.

▶ Last admission is 45 minutes before closing.

✗ Take a Break

The **Tea Rooms at Edinburgh Castle** (Crown Sq; mains £7-15; ⊙10am-5pm) serves good lunches made with fresh Scottish produce. Or just a few yards downhill from the castle on the Royal Mile, there's Amber (p45) and Witchery by the Castle (p45).

Understand
Stone of Destiny
----- ----- ----- -----

On St Andrew's Day 1996, with much pomp and ceremony, a block of sandstone 26.5 inches by 16.5 inches by 11 inches in size (67cm by 42cm by 28cm), with rusted iron hoops at either end, was installed in Edinburgh Castle. For the previous 700 years it had lain beneath the Coronation Chair in London's Westminster Abbey, where almost every English, and later British, monarch from Edward II in 1308 to Elizabeth II in 1953 had sat during their coronation ceremonies.

This is the legendary Stone of Destiny, on which Scottish kings placed their feet during their coronation (not their bums; the English got that bit wrong). It was stolen from Scone Abbey near Perth by King Edward I of England in 1296 and taken to London where it remained for seven centuries, an enduring symbol of Scotland's subjugation by England.

It returned to the political limelight in 1996, when the Westminster government arranged for its return in an attempt to boost the flagging popularity of the Conservative Party in Scotland prior to a general election. (The stunt failed – Scotland returned no Conservative MPs at the ensuing election.)

at the order of Queen Victoria; it was rededicated in 1934. The tiny **stained-glass windows** – depicting Margaret, St Andrew, St Columba, St Ninian and William Wallace – date from the 1920s.

Mons Meg
Immediately north of St Margaret's Chapel is **Mons Meg**, a giant 15th-century siege gun built at Mons in Belgium in 1449. The gun was last fired in 1681, as a birthday salute for the future King James VII/II, when its barrel burst. Take a peek over the wall to the north of the chapel and you'll see a charming little garden that was used as a **pet cemetery** for officers' dogs.

Great Hall
The main group of buildings on the summit of Castle Rock are ranged around Crown Sq, dominated by the shrine of the **Scottish National War Memorial**. Opposite is the **Great Hall**, built for James IV (r 1488–1513) as a ceremonial hall and used as a meeting place for the Scottish parliament until 1639. Its most remarkable feature is the original 16th-century hammer-beam roof.

Prisons of War Exhibition
The **Castle Vaults** beneath the Great Hall (entered on the west side of Crown Sq) were used variously as storerooms, bakeries and prisons. The vaults have been restored to how they were in the 18th and early 19th centuries, when they were used as a prison

Edinburgh Castle

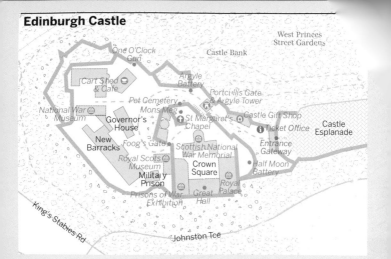

for soldiers captured during the American War of Independence and the Napoleonic Wars. Original graffiti carved by French and American prisoners can be seen on the ancient wooden doors

Honours of Scotland

The **Royal Palace**, built during the 15th and 16th centuries, houses a series of historical tableaux leading to the highlight of the castle – a strongroom housing the **Honours of Scotland** (the Scottish Crown Jewels), the oldest surviving Crown Jewels

in Europe. Locked away in a chest following the Act of Union in 1707, the crown (made in 1540 from the gold of Robert the Bruce's 14th-century coronet), sword and sceptre lay forgotten until they were unearthed at the instigation of the novelist Sir Walter Scott in 1818. Also on display here is the **Stone of Destiny**.

Among the neighbouring **Royal Apartments** is the bedchamber where Mary, Queen of Scots gave birth to her son James VI, who was to unite the crowns of Scotland and England in 1603.

Top Sights
Real Mary King's Close

Edinburgh's 18th-century city chambers were built over the sealed-off remains of Mary King's Close, and the lower levels of this medieval Old Town alley have survived almost unchanged amid the foundations for 250 years. Now open to the public, this spooky, subterranean labyrinth gives a fascinating insight into the everyday life of 17th-century Edinburgh. A costumed drama student in period costume will take you on a guided tour through the vaults, while practising his or her dramatic enunciation.

👁 Map p36, D3

📞0845 070 6244

www.realmarykingsclose.com

2 Warriston's Close, High St

adult/child £12.95/7.45

🕙10am-9pm daily Apr-Oct, to 11pm Aug

Don't Miss

The Tenement Room

The scripted tour provided by your costumed guide, complete with ghostly tales and gruesome tableaux, can seem a little naff, milking the scary and scatological aspects of the close's history for all they're worth. But there are many things of genuine interest to see; there's something about the crumbling 17th-century tenement room that makes the hairs rise on the back of your neck, with tufts of horsehair poking from the collapsing lath-and-plaster walls, the ghost of a pattern on the walls, and the ancient smell of stone and dust thick in your nostrils.

Wee Annie's Room

In one of the former bedrooms off the close, a psychic once claimed to have been approached by the ghost of a little girl called Annie. It's hard to tell what's more frightening – the story of the ghostly child, or the bizarre heap of tiny dolls and teddies left in a corner by sympathetic visitors.

The Foot of the Close

Perhaps the most atmospheric part of the tour is at the end, when you stand at the foot of Mary King's Close itself. You are effectively standing in a buried street with the old tenement walls rising on either side, and the weight of the 11 storeys of the city chambers above – and some 250 years of history – pressing down all around you.

☑ Top Tips

▶ From November to March, opening hours are 10am to 5pm Sunday to Thursday, to 9pm Friday and Saturday.

▶ Tours are limited to 20 people at a time, so book online at least 48 hours in advance to secure a place; to book within 48 hours, phone.

▶ The tour includes stairs and uneven stone surfaces – wear suitable shoes.

▶ There are lots of enclosed spaces – not recommended if you suffer from claustrophobia!

▶ Children under the age of five are not admitted.

✗ Take a Break

Enjoy pizza at a pavement table at **Gordon's Trattoria** (www.gordonstrattoriaedinburgh.co.uk; 231 High St; ⊙noon-midnight Sun-Thu, to 3am Fri & Sat; ▣all South Bridge buses), a short distance downhill; or a more sophisticated seafood lunch at Ondine (p44), uphill and round the corner.

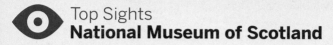

Top Sights
National Museum of Scotland

The golden stone and striking modern architecture of the National Museum's new building, opened in 1998, make it one of the city's most distinctive landmarks. The five floors of the museum trace the history of Scotland from geological beginnings to the 1990s. The new building connects with the original Victorian museum, which underwent a major revamp in 2011; it covers natural history, archaeology, scientific and industrial technology, and the decorative arts of ancient Egypt, Islam and the Orient.

Map p36, E4

www.nms.ac.uk

Chambers St

fee for special exhibitions

⊙10am-5pm

Don't Miss

Grand Gallery

The museum's main entrance, in the middle of Chambers St, leads into an atmospheric entrance hall occupying what used to be the museum cellars. Stairs lead up into the light of the Victorian **Grand Gallery**, a spectacular glass-roofed atrium lined with cast-iron pillars and balconies; this was the centrepiece of the original Victorian museum. It was designed in the 1860s by Captain Francis Fowke of the Royal Engineers, who also created the Royal Albert Hall in London, and parts of London's Victoria and Albert Museum.

Crowds gather on the hour to watch the chiming of the **Millennium Clock Tower**. Built in 1999 to commemorate the best and worst of human history, and inspired by mechanical marvels such as Prague's Astronomical Clock, it is more of a kinetic sculpture than a clock, crammed with amusing and thought-provoking symbols and animated figures.

Animal World

A door at the east end of the Grand Gallery leads into Animal World, one of the most impressive of the Victorian museum's new exhibits. No dusty, static regiments of stuffed creatures here, but a beautiful and dynamic display of animals apparently caught in the act of bounding, leaping or pouncing, arranged in groups that illustrate different means of locomotion, methods of feeding and modes of reproduction. Extinct creatures, including a full-size skeleton of Tyrannosaurus rex, mingle with the living.

Window on the World

The exhibits ranged around the balconies of the Grand Gallery are billed as a 'Window on the

☑ **Top Tips**

▶ Begin at the main entrance in the middle of Chambers St, rather than the modern tower at the west end of the street. You'll find an info desk with museum maps and leaflets, a cloakroom, toilets and a cafe·restaurant.

▶ Free, one-hour guided tours of the museum depart at 11am, 1pm and 3pm, each covering a different theme; ask for details at the info desk.

▶ You can download PDFs of museum trails for children to follow.

✕ **Take a Break**

The **Museum Brasserie** (☎ 225 4040; Chambers St; mains £6-8; ⊙10am-5pm; ♿) in the basement of the Victorian part of the museum serves light lunches; Tower (p45), in the modern half, is more formal and has an outdoor terrace with stunning views over the city.

...d' that showcases more than 800
...ns from the museum's collections,
...nging from the **world's largest scrim-shaw carving**, occupying two full-size
sperm whale jawbones, to a four-seat
racing bicycle dating from 1898.

Hawthornden Court

At the west end of the Grand Gallery,
the Connect exhibit showcases **Dolly
the Sheep**, the world's first mammal
cloned from an adult cell, and leads
into Hawthornden Court, the soaring
central atrium of the modern half of
the museum, graced by the **Formula 1
racing car** driven by Sir Jackie Stewart
(Scotland's most successful racing
driver) in the 1970s.

Early People Gallery

Stairs at the far end of Hawthornden
Court lead down to the Early People
Gallery on level 0, decorated with
intriguing humanoid sculptures by Sir
Eduardo Paolozzi and beautiful instal-
lations by sculptor Andy Galsworthy,
including huge stacks of old roofing
slates, cleverly arranged scrap timber
and a sphere made entirely of whale
bones. Look for the **Cramond Lioness**,
a Roman funerary sculpture of a lion
gripping a human head in her jaws (it
was discovered in the River Almond,
on the western edge of Edinburgh, in
1997), and the 22kg of Roman silver
that makes up the **Traprain Treasure**.
It was buried in the 5th century AD
and discovered in 1919, and is the
biggest known hoard of Roman silver
ever to be found.

Kingdom of the Scots

From the Early People Gallery, you
work your way upwards through the
history of Scotland. Highlights of
the medieval Kingdom of the Scots
galleries, on levels 1 and 2, include the
Monymusk Reliquary, a tiny silver cas-
ket dating from AD 750, which is said
to have been carried into battle with
Robert the Bruce at Bannockburn in
1314; and the famous **Lewis Chessmen**, a set of charming 12th-century
chess pieces carved from walrus ivory,
that was discovered on Uig beach on
the Isle of Lewis.

Daith Comes In...

The Daith Comes In (Death Comes In)
exhibit on level 5 is a goth's paradise
of wooden hearses, jet jewellery and
mourning bracelets made from human
hair, as well as the 'mortsafes' that
once protected newly buried corpses
from the ravages of the bodysnatchers.
But the most fascinating objects
on display here are the mysterious
Arthur's Seat coffins. Discovered by
two boys playing in a cave in Holyrood
Park in 1836, these 17 miniature coffins, less than 4 inches (10cm) long –
complete with tiny wooden figures
inside – may have been a mock burial
for the victims of Edinburgh's most
famous bodysnatchers, Burke and
Hare, who sold their murdered victims to the city's anatomy professor;
for more see p44.

Leaving Scotland

Level 6 of the museum is given over to the 20th century, with galleries devoted to war, industry and daily life illustrated by personal stories, film clips and iconic objects such as a set of bagpipes that was played at the Battle of the Somme in 1916. There is also a particularly affecting exhibition called Leaving Scotland, containing stories of the Scottish diaspora that emigrated to begin new lives in Canada, Australia, the USA and other places, from the 18th century right up until the 1960s.

Roof Terrace

Before you leave, find the elevator in the corner of level 6 near the war gallery and go up to the roof terrace to enjoy a fantastic view across the city to the castle ramparts.

Local Life
Explore the Old Town's Hidden History

Edinburgh's Old Town extends to the south of the Royal Mile, descending into the the valley of the Grassmarket and Cowgate, which is crossed by the arches of George IV Bridge and South Bridge. This difference in levels has created a maze of narrow closes, wynds and staircases, which lend an adventurous air to exploring its many hidden corners.

① Victoria Terrace

From the Lawnmarket at the top of the Royal Mile, dive down Fisher's Close, which leads you onto the delightful Victoria Terrace, strung above the cobbled curve of shop-lined Victoria St. Wander along to the right, enjoying the view – **Maxie's Bistro** (☎226 7770; www.maxiesbistro.com; 5b Johnston Tce; mains £10-22; ☺11am-11pm; 🚌2, 23, 27, 41, 42, 45), at the far end of the terrace, is a great place to stop for lunch or a drink.

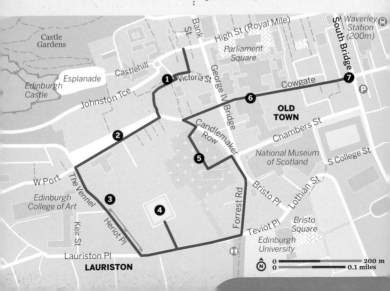

❷ Grassmarket

Descend the stairs in the middle of the terrace and continue downhill to the Grassmarket. The site of a cattle market from the 15th century until the start of the 20th, the Grassmarket was also the city's place of execution, and martyred Covenanters are commemorated by a monument at the eastern end, where the gallows once stood. The notorious murderers Burke and Hare operated from a now-vanished close off the west end.

❸ Flodden Wall

Turn left up the flight of stairs known as the Vennel. At the top of the steps on the left you'll find the Flodden Wall, one of the few surviving fragments of the city wall that was built in the early 16th century as protection against a feared English invasion. Beyond it stretches the Telfer Wall, a later extension.

❹ George Heriot's School

Turn left along Lauriston Pl to find George Heriot's School, one of the most impressive buildings in the Old Town. Built in the 17th century with funds bequeathed by George Heriot (goldsmith and banker to King James VI, and popularly known as Jinglin' Geordie), it was originally a school for orphaned children, but became a fee-paying school in 1886. It is open to the public on Doors Open Day (www.doorsopendays.org.uk) in September.

❺ Greyfriars Kirkyard

Hemmed in by high walls and overlooked by the castle, Greyfriars Kirkyard is one of Edinburgh's most evocative spots, a peaceful green oasis dotted with elaborate monuments. Many famous Edinburgh names are buried here, including poet Allan Ramsay (1686–1758), and William Smellie (1740–95), editor of the first edition of Encyclopaedia Britannica.

❻ Cowgate

The Cowgate – the long, dark ravine leading eastwards from the Grassmarket – was once the road along which cattle were driven from the pastures around Arthur's Seat to the safety of the city walls, or to be sold at market. To the right are the new law courts, followed by Tailors Hall (built 1621, extended 1757), now a hotel and bar but formerly the meeting place of the 'Companie of Tailzeours' (Tailors' Guild).

❼ South Bridge Vaults

South Bridge passes over the Cowgate in a single arch, but there are another nine arches hidden on either side, surrounded by later buildings. The ones to the north can be visited on a guided tour with Mercat Tours (p152); those to the south are occupied by a nightclub, The Caves (p49).

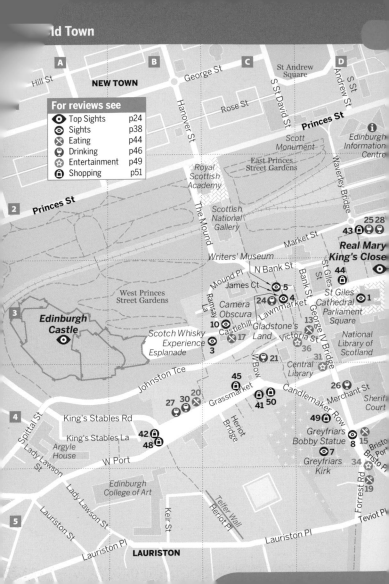

A   **B**   **C**   **D**

Hill St

NEW TOWN

George St

St Andrew Square

S St Andrew St

Rose St

S St David St

Hanover St

Princes St

Scott Monument

Waverley Bridge

ⓘ Edinburgh Information Centre

Royal Scottish Academy

East Princes Street Gardens

2   Princes St

The Mound

Scottish National Gallery

Market St

25 28

43 ⬢ ◎ ◎

Real Mary King's Close ◉

Writers' Museum

Mound Pl   N Bank St

James Ct   ◎ 5

Ramsay La   Bank St

St Giles St

44 ⬢

St Giles Cathedral ◎ 1

West Princes Street Gardens

Camera Obscura

24 ◎ ◎ 4

Lawnmarket

George IV Bridge

Parliament Square

3   **Edinburgh Castle** ◉

Scotch Whisky Experience   10 ◎

Castlehill

Gladstone's Land

13 ◎

National Library of Scotland

Esplanade   ✗ 17

3

Victoria St

36 ◎

W Bow   🍷 21

Central Library

31 ★

26 🍷

Merchant St

Johnston Tce

45 ⬢

Candlemaker Row

Sheriff Court

27   30   20

🍷   ◎

Grassmarket

41   50

⬢ ⬢

Heriot Bridge

49 ⬢

Greyfriars Bobby Statue ◎ 8

Bristo Por

Bristo

4   Spittal St

King's Stables Rd

King's Stables La   42 ⬢

48 ⬢

Lady Lawson St

Argyle House

W Port

15

7 ◎

Greyfriars Kirk

34 ⬢

Forrest Rd

19 ✗

Lady Lawson St

Edinburgh College of Art

Keir St

Heriot Wall

Teviot Pl

5   Lauriston St

Lauriston Pl

Telfer Wall

Lauriston Pl

LAURISTON

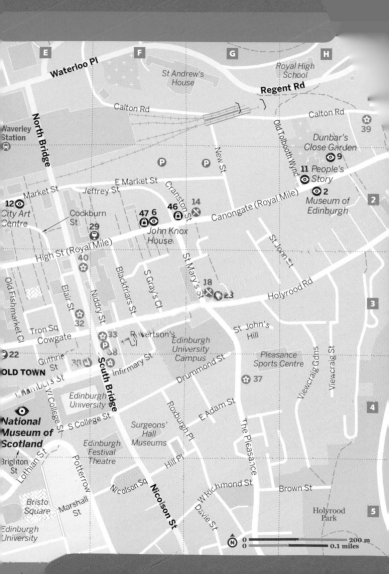

ghts

t Giles Cathedral CHURCH

1 ⊙ Map p36, D3

Properly called the High Kirk of Edinburgh (it was only a true cathedral – the seat of a bishop – from 1633 to 1638 and from 1661 to 1689), St Giles Cathedral is named after the patron saint of cripples and beggars. The present church dates largely from the 15th century – the beautiful crown spire was completed in 1495 – but much of it was restored in the 19th century.

The cathedral occupies the site of a Norman-style church that was built in 1126 but destroyed by English invaders in 1385; the only substantial remains are the central piers that support the tower. The present-day interior lacks grandeur but is rich in history: St Giles was at the heart of the Scottish Reformation, and John Knox served as minister here from 1559 to 1572. One of the most interesting corners of the kirk is the Thistle Chapel, built in 1911 for the Knights of the Most Ancient & Most Noble Order of the Thistle. The elaborately carved Gothic-style stalls have canopies topped with the helms and arms of the 16 knights – look out for the bagpipe-playing angel amid the vaulting. Outside the eastern end of St Giles is the **Mercat Cross**, a 19th-century copy of the 1365 original, where merchants and traders met to

St Giles Cathedral

CHRIS HEPBURN/GETTY IMAGES ©

Understand

Old Town History

Before the founding of the New Town in the 18th century, old Edinburgh was an overcrowded and unsanitary hive of humanity. Constrained between the boggy ground of the Nor' Loch (now drained and occupied by Princes Street Gardens) to the north and the city walls to the south and east, the only way for the town to expand was upwards.

Old Town Tenements

The five- to eight-storey tenements that were raised along the Royal Mile in the 16th and 17th centuries were the skyscrapers of their day, remarked upon with wonder by visiting writers such as Daniel Defoe. All classes of society, from beggars to magistrates, lived cheek by jowl in these urban ants' nests, the wealthy occupying the middle floors – high enough to be above the noise and stink of the streets, but not so high that climbing the stairs would be too tiring – while the poor squeezed into attics, basements, cellars and vaults.

Royal Mile

The Royal Mile, Edinburgh's oldest street, connects the castle to the Palace of Holyroodhouse. It is split into four named sections: Castlehill, the Lawnmarket, the High St and the Canongate.

A corruption of 'Landmarket', **Lawnmarket** takes its name from a large cloth market (selling goods from the land outside the city) that flourished here until the 18th century; this was the poshest part of the Old Town, where many distinguished citizens made their homes.

High Street, which stretches from George IV Bridge down to St Mary's St, is the heart and soul of the Old Town, home to the city's main church, the law courts, the city chambers and – until 1707 – the Scottish parliament. It ends at St Mary St, where the Old Town's eastern gate, the Netherbow Port (part of the Flodden Wall), once stood. Though it no longer exists, its former outline is marked by brass strips set in the road.

Canongate – the section between the Netherbow and Holyrood – takes its name from the Augustinian canons (monks) of Holyrood Abbey. From the 16th century it was home to aristocrats who wanted to live near the Palace of Holyroodhouse.

...business and royal proclama-
...ere read; in 1745, Bonnie Prince
...e had his father proclaimed King
...es VIII of Scotland here.

...Outside the western door is a cob-
...blestone heart set into the paving that
marks the site of the 15th-century **Tolbooth**. The Tolbooth served variously
as a meeting place for parliament and
the town council before becoming law
courts and, finally, a notorious prison
and place of execution. Immortalised
in Sir Walter Scott's novel *The Heart of
Midlothian*, the Tolbooth was demolished in the 19th century. Passersby
traditionally spit on the heart for good
luck (don't stand downwind!). (www.
stgilescathedral.org.uk; High St; suggested

☑ Top Tip
Parliament Hall
Before you visit the Scottish Parliament Building, take a look at the
magnificent 17th-century **Parliament Hall** (Map p36, D3; 11 Parliament
Sq; admission free; ⊙10am-4pm Mon-Fri;
🚍2, 23, 27, 41, 42, 45). Tucked behind
St Giles Cathedral, it has an original
oak hammer-beam roof, and is
where the original Scottish parliament met before its dissolution in
1707. Now used by lawyers and their
clients as a meeting place, it's open
to the public. As you enter (there's
a sign outside saying 'Parliament
Hall; Court of Session') you'll see
the reception desk in front of you;
the hall is through the double doors
immediately on your right.

---

donation £3; ⊙9am-7pm Mon-Fri, to 5pm Sat,
1-5pm Sun May-Sep, 9am-5pm Mon-Sat, 1-5pm
Sun Oct-Apr; 🚍2, 23, 27, 41, 42, 45)

Museum of Edinburgh   MUSEUM

2 ◎ Map p36, H2

You can't miss the colourful facade
of Huntly House, newly renovated in
bright red and yellow ochre, opposite
the Tolbooth clock. Built in 1570, it
houses a museum covering Edinburgh
from its prehistory to the present. Exhibits of national importance include
an original copy of the National Covenant of 1638, but the big crowd-pleaser
is the dog collar and feeding bowl that
once belonged to Greyfriars Bobby
(p42), the city's most famous canine
citizen. (www.edinburghmuseums.org.uk; 142
Canongate; admission free; ⊙10am-5pm Mon-
Sat year-round, 2-5pm Sun Aug; 🚍35)

Scotch Whisky Experience   EXHIBITION

3 ◎ Map p36, C3

A former school houses this multimedia centre explaining the making of
whisky from barley to bottle in a series
of exhibits, demonstrations and tours
that combine sight, sound, taste and
smell, including the world's largest collection of malt whiskies; look out for
Peat the distillery cat! More expensive
tours include more extensive whisky
tastings and samples of Scottish
cuisine. (www.scotchwhiskyexperience.co.uk;
354 Castlehill; adult/child incl tour & tasting
£12.75/6.50; ⊙10am-6.30pm Jun-Aug, to 6pm
Sep-May; 🚍2, 23, 27, 41, 42, 45)

Understand
Underground Edinburgh

As Edinburgh expanded in the late 18th and early 19th centuries, new bridges were built to link the Old Town to newly built areas to its north and south. **South Bridge** (completed 1788) and **George IV Bridge** (1834) lead southwards from the Royal Mile over the deep valley of the Cowgate, but since their construction so many buildings have clustered around them that you can hardly tell they are bridges: George IV Bridge has a total of nine arches but only two are visible, and South Bridge has no less than 18 hidden arches.

These underground vaults were originally used as storerooms, workshops and drinking dens. But as early 19th-century Edinburgh's population swelled with an influx of penniless Highlanders cleared from their lands and Irish refugees from the potato famine, the dark, dripping chambers were given over to slum accommodation. The vaults were eventually cleared in the late 19th century, then lay forgotten until 1994 when some of the South Bridge vaults were opened to guided tours (from Mercat Tours, p35), while others are now home to atmospheric nightclubs such as Cabaret Voltaire (p49) and The Caves (p49).

Gladstone's Land   HISTORIC BUILDING

4 ◉ Map p36, C3

One of Edinburgh's most prominent 17th-century merchants was Thomas Gledstanes, who in 1617 purchased the tenement later known as Gladstone's Land. It contains fine painted ceilings, walls and beams, and some splendid furniture from the 17th and 18th centuries. The volunteer guides provide a wealth of anecdotes and a detailed history. (NTS; www.nts.org.uk; 477 Lawnmarket; adult/child £6.50/5; ⊙10am-6.30pm Jul & Aug, to 5pm Apr-Jun & Sep-Oct; ◻2, 23, 27, 41, 42, 45)

Writers' Museum   MUSEUM

5 ◉ Map p36, C3

Tucked down a close just east of Gladstone's Land you'll find Lady Stair's House (1622), home to this museum that contains manuscripts and memorabilia belonging to three of Scotland's most famous writers: Robert Burns, Sir Walter Scott and Robert Louis Stevenson. (www.edinburghmuseums.org.uk; Lady Stair's Close, Lawnmarket; admission free; ⊙10am-5pm Mon-Sat year-round, 2-5pm Sun Aug; ◻23, 27, 41, 42)

Local Life
Edinburgh's Mysterious Book Sculptures

In 2011–12 an unknown artist left a series of paper sculptures in various Edinburgh libraries, museums and bookshops. Each was fashioned from an old book and alluded to literary themes; an anonymous message from the artist revealed they had been inspired by the poem 'Gifts', by Edinburgh poet Norman McCaig. Two are on display at the **Scottish Poetry Library** (Map p36, H2; www.spl.org.uk; 5 Crichton's Close, Canongate; admission free; ⊘10am-5pm Tue, Wed & Fri, to 7pm Thu, to 4pm Sat; 🚇35, 36) where you can pick up a self-guided walking-tour leaflet (also available on its website).

John Knox House   HISTORIC BUILDING

6 ◉ Map p36, F2

This is the oldest surviving tenement in Edinburgh, dating from around 1490. John Knox, an influential church reformer and leader of the Protestant Reformation in Scotland, is thought to have lived here from 1561 to 1572. The labyrinthine interior has some beautiful painted-timber ceilings and an interesting exhibition on Knox's life and work. (www.scottishstorytelling centre.co.uk; 43-45 High St; adult/child £5/1; ⊘10am-6pm Mon-Sat year-round, noon-6pm Sun Jul & Aug; 🚇35)

Greyfriars Kirk   CHURCH

7 ◉ Map p36, D4

One of Edinburgh's most famous churches, Greyfriars Kirk was built on the site of a Franciscan friary and opened for worship on Christmas Day 1620. In 1638 the National Covenant was signed here, rejecting Charles I's attempts to impose episcopacy and a new English prayer book on the Scots, and affirming the independence of the Scottish Church. Many who signed were later executed at the Grassmarket and, in 1679, 1200 Covenanters were held prisoner in terrible conditions in the southwestern corner of the kirkyard. There's a small exhibition inside the church. (www.greyfriarskirk.com; Candlemaker Row; admission free; ⊘10.30am-4.30pm Mon-Fri & 11am-2pm Sat Apr-Oct, closed Nov-Mar; 🚇2, 23, 27, 41, 42 or 45)

Greyfriars Bobby Statue   MONUMENT

8 ◉ Map p36, D4

This tiny statue is a memorial to Greyfriars Bobby, a Skye terrier who, from 1858 to 1872, maintained a vigil over the grave of his master, an Edinburgh police officer. The story was immortalised in a novel by Eleanor Atkinson in 1912, and in 1963 was made into a movie by – who else? – Walt Disney. Bobby's own grave, marked by a small, pink granite stone, is just inside the entrance to Greyfriars Kirkyard. You can see his original collar and bowl in the Museum of Edinburgh (p40).

(cnr George IV Bridge & Candlemaker Row; 🚌 2, 23, 27, 41, 42 or 45)

Dunbar's Close Garden GARDENS

9 ◎ Map p36, H2

Tucked away at the end of an Old Town close, this walled garden has been laid out in the style of the 17th century, with gravel paths, neatly trimmed shrubs, herbs and flowers and mature trees. A hidden gem, and an oasis of tranquillity amid the bustle of the Royal Mile. (Canongate; ⏱24hr; 🚌35)

Camera Obscura EXHIBITION

10 ◎ Map p36, C3

Edinburgh's camera obscura is a curious 19th-century device in constant use since 1853 – that uses lenses and mirrors to throw a live image of the city onto a large horizontal screen. The accompanying commentary is entertaining and the whole experience has a quirky charm, complemented by an intriguing exhibition dedicated to illusions of all kinds. Stairs lead up through various displays to the **Outlook Tower**, which offers great views over the city. (www.camera-obscura.co.uk; Castlehill; adult/child £11.95/8.95; ⏱9.30am-9pm Jul & Aug, to 7pm Apr-Jun & Sep-Oct, 10am-6pm Nov-Mar; 🚌2)

People's Story MUSEUM

11 ◎ Map p36, H2

One of the surviving symbols of Canongate's former independence is the **Canongate Tolbooth**. Built in 1591, it served successively as a collection point for tolls (taxes), a council house, a courtroom and a jail. It now houses a fascinating museum called the People's Story, which covers the life, work and pastimes of ordinary Edinburgh folk from the 18th century to today. (www.edinburghmuseums.org.uk; 163 Canongate; admission free; ⏱10am-5pm Mon-Sat year-round, 2-5pm Sun Aug; 🚌35)

City Art Centre ART CENTRE

12 ◎ Map p36, E2

The largest and most populist of Edinburgh's smaller galleries, the CAC is home to the city's collection

John Knox portrait, inside John Knox House

Understand
The Resurrection Men

Edinburgh has long had a reputation for being at the cutting edge of medical research. In the early 19th century this led to a shortage of cadavers with which the city's anatomists could satisfy their curiosity, and an illegal trade in dead bodies emerged.

The readiest supply of corpses was to be found in the city's graveyards. Grave robbers – known as 'resurrection men' – plundered newly buried coffins and sold the cadavers to the anatomists, who turned a blind eye to the source of their research material.

William Burke and William Hare took the bodysnatching business a step further, deciding to create their own supply of fresh cadavers by resorting to murder. Between December 1827 and October 1828 they killed at least 16 people, selling their bodies to the surgeon Robert Knox.

When the law finally caught up with them Hare testified against Burke, who was hanged outside St Giles Cathedral in January 1829. In an ironic twist, his body was given to the anatomy school for public dissection.

of Scottish art, ranging from the 17th century to the 20th (including works by the Scottish Colourists), as well as many fine paintings, engravings and photographs showing views of Edinburgh at various stages of its history. (www.edinburghmuseums.org.uk; 2 Market St; fee for temporary exhibitions; ⏰10am-5pm Mon-Sat, noon-5pm Sun; 🚌36)

Eating

Ondine   SEAFOOD £££
13 ✗ Map p36, D3

Ondine is one of Edinburgh's finest seafood restaurants, with a menu based on sustainably sourced fish. Take an octopus-inspired seat at the curved Crustacean Bar and tuck into oysters Kilpatrick, a roast shellfish platter, the crunchiest calamari ever, or good old haddock and chips (with minted pea purée, just to keep things posh). The two-course lunch (noon to 2.30pm) and pre-theatre menu (5.30pm to 6.30pm) costs £18. (✆226 1888; www.ondinerestaurant.co.uk; 2 George IV Bridge; mains £15-28; ⏰lunch & dinner Mon-Sat; 🚌2, 23, 27, 41, 42, 45)

Wedgwood   SCOTTISH £££
14 ✗ Map p36, G2

Fine food without the fuss is the motto at this friendly and unpretentious restaurant. Scottish produce is served with an inventive flair in dishes such as wild venison with its own haggis, herbed barley and a truffled jus, while the menu includes foraged wild salad leaves collected by the chef himself. (📞558 8737; www.wedgwoodthe restaurant.co.uk; 267 Canongate; mains £16-27, 2-/3-course lunch £12/16; ☺lunch & dinner; 🚌35)

Tower
SCOTTISH £££

15 Map p36, D4

Chic and sleek, with a great view of the castle, Tower is perched in a turret atop the National Museum of Scotland building. A star-studded guest list of celebrities has enjoyed its menu of quality Scottish food, simply prepared – try half a dozen oysters followed by roast partridge with chestnut stuffing. A two-/three-course pre-theatre menu (£16/22) is available from 5pm to 6.30pm, and afternoon tea (from £16) is served from 2pm to 5pm. (📞225 3003; www.tower-restaurant. com; National Museum of Scotland, Chambers St; mains £18-34; ☺10am-11pm; 🚌2, 23, 27, 41, 42, 45)

Witchery by the Castle
SCOTTISH/FRENCH £££

17 Map p36, C3

Set in a merchant's town house dating from 1595, the Witchery is a candlelit corner of antique splendour with oak-panelled walls, low ceilings, wall hangings and red leather ...stery; stairs lead down to a seco... even more romantic, dining room... called the Secret Garden. The men... ranges from foie gras to Aberdeen Angus steak and the wine list runs to almost 1000 bins. (📞225 5613; Castlehill; mains £23-35, 2-course lunch £16; ☺noon-4pm & 5.30-11.30pm; 🚌2, 23, 27, 41, 42)

David Bann
VEGETARIAN £

18 Map p36, G3

If you want to convince a carnivorous friend that cuisine à la veg can be as tasty and inventive as a meat-muncher's menu, take them to David Bann's stylish restaurant. Dishes such as mushroom strudel with celeriac sauce and dauphinois potatoes, and Thai fritter of spiced broccoli and smoked tofu, are guaranteed to win converts. (📞556 5888; www.davidbann. com; 56-58 St Mary's St; mains £9-13; ☺noon-10pm Mon-Fri, 11am-10pm Sat & Sun; 🍴; 🚌35)

Amber
SCOTTISH ££

You've got to love a place where the waiter greets you with the words, 'My name is Craig, and I'll be your whisky adviser for this evening.' Located in

Whisky Experience (see ...36, C3), this whisky-themed ...nt manages to avoid the ...clichés and creates genuinely ...resting dishes such as mussels ...an Islay whisky cream sauce, and sirloin steak with thyme-roasted potatoes and whisky butter. (☑477 8477; www.amber-restaurant.co.uk; 354 Castlehill; mains £12-20; ☺10am-7.30pm Sun-Thu, to 9pm Fri-Sat; ☒2, 23, 27, 41, 42, 45)

Mums

CAFE £

19 🍴 Map p36, D5

This nostalgia-fuelled cafe serves up classic British comfort food that wouldn't look out of place on a 1950s menu – bacon and eggs, bangers and mash, shepherd's pie, fish and chips. But there's a twist – the food is all top-quality nosh freshly prepared from local produce. There's even a wine list, though we prefer the real ales and Scottish-brewed cider. (www.monstermashcafe.co.uk; 4a Forrest Rd; mains £6-9; ☺9am-10pm Mon-Sat, 10am-10pm Sun; ☒2, 23, 27, 41, 42, 45)

Petit Paris

FRENCH ££

20 🍴 Map p36, B4

Like the name says, this is a little piece of Paris, complete with checked tablecloths, friendly waiters and good-value grub – the *moules-frites* (mussels and chips) is excellent. There's a lunch/pre-theatre deal (noon to 3pm and 5.30pm to 7pm) offering the *plat du jour* and a coffee for £8; add a starter and it's £12. (☑226 2442; www.

petitparis-restaurant.co.uk; 38-40 Grassmarket; mains £14-18; ☺noon-3pm & 5.30-11pm, closed Mon Oct-Mar; ☒2)

Drinking

Bow Bar

PUB

21 🍺 Map p36, C3

One of the city's best traditional-style pubs (it's not as old as it looks), serving a range of excellent real ales and a vast selection of malt whiskies and designer gins, the Bow Bar often has standing room only on Friday and Saturday evenings. (80 West Bow; ☒2, 23, 27, 41, 42, 45)

BrewDog

BAR

22 🍺 Map p36, E4

A new bar from Scotland's self-styled 'punk brewery', BrewDog stands out

---

☑ Top Tip

Ghost Tours

The City of the Dead tour (p152) of Greyfriars Kirkyard, run by Black Hart Storytellers, is probably the scariest of Edinburgh's ghost tours. Many people have reported encounters with the 'McKenzie Poltergeist', the ghost of a 17th-century judge who persecuted the Covenanters, and now haunts their former prison in a corner of the kirkyard. Not suitable for young children!

WILL ROBB/GETTY IMAGES ©

BrewDog

among the grimy, sticky-floored dives that line the Cowgate, with its cool, industrial-chic designer look. As well as its own highly rated beers, there's a choice of four guest real ales. (www.brewdog.com; 143 Cowgate; 🛜; 🚌36)

Holyrood 9A PUB

24 🍷 Map p36, G3

Candlelight flickering off hectares of polished wood creates an atmospheric setting for this superb real-ale bar, with no fewer than 20 taps pouring craft beers from all corners of the country. If you're peckish, it serves excellent gourmet burgers, too. (www.fullerthomson.com; 9a Holyrood Rd; 🛜; 🚌36)

Jolly Judge PUB

24 🍷 Map p36, C3

A snug little howff (a Scots word for a favourite haunt or meeting place) tucked away down a close, the Judge exudes a cosy 17th-century atmosphere (low, timber beamed painted ceilings) and has the added attraction of a cheering open fire in cold weather. No music or gaming machines, just the buzz of conversation. (www.jollyjudge.co.uk; 7a James Ct; 🛜; 🚌2, 23, 27, 41, 42, 45)

Ecco Vino WINE BAR

25 🍷 Map p36, D2

With outdoor tables on sunny afternoons, and cosy candlelit intimacy

Bow Bar (p46)

in the evenings, this comfortably cramped Tuscan-style wine bar offers a tempting range of Italian wines, though not all are available by the glass – best to share a bottle. (www.eccovinoedinburgh.com; 19 Cockburn St; 📶; 🚌36, 41)

Villager

BAR

26 🍺 Map p36, D4

A cross between a traditional pub and a pre-club bar, Villager has a comfortable, laid-back vibe. It can be standing room only in the main bar in the evenings (the cocktails are excellent), but the side room, with its brown leather sofas and subtropical pot

plants, comes into its own for a lazy Sunday afternoon with the papers. (www.villagerbar.com; 49-50 George IV Bridge; 📶; 🚌2, 23, 27, 41, 42, 45)

Beehive Inn

PUB

27 🍺 Map p36, B4

The historic Beehive, a former coaching inn, is a big, buzzing party pub, with a range of real ales, but the main attraction is sitting out the back in the Grassmarket's only beer garden, with views up to the castle. (18-20 Grassmarket; 🚌2)

Malt Shovel

PUB

28 🍺 Map p36, D2

A traditional-looking pub with dark wood and subdued tartanry, the Malt Shovel offers a good range of real ales and more than 100 malt whiskies, and is famed for its regular Tuesday-night jazz and Thursday-night folk-music sessions. (📞225 6843; www.taylor-walker.co.uk; 11-15 Cockburn St; 📶👶; 🚌36, 41)

Royal Mile Tavern

PUB

29 🍺 Map p36, F2

An elegant, traditional bar lined with polished wood, mirrors and brass, Royal Mile serves real ale (Deuchars IPA and Caledonian 80/-), good wines and decent pub grub – fish and chips, steak and Guinness pie, sausage and mash etc. Live music from 9pm every night. (www.royalmiletavern.com; 127 High St; 🚌35)

White Hart Inn PUB

30 ⊖ Map p36, B4

A brass plaque outside this pub proclaims: 'In the White Hart Inn Robert Burns stayed during his last visit to Edinburgh, 1791.' Claiming to be the city's oldest pub in continuous use (since 1516), it also hosted William Wordsworth in 1803. Not surprisingly, it's a traditional, cosy, low-raftered place. It has folk/acoustic music sessions every night. (☎226 2806; www.whitehart-edinburgh.co.uk; 34 Grassmarket; ☒2)

Entertainment

Bongo Club CLUB

31 ✪ Map p36, D4

The weird and wonderful Bongo Club boasts a long history of hosting everything from wild club nights to performance art to kids' comedy shows, and is open as a cafe and exhibition space during the day. Now settling into a new venue beneath the

---

☑ Top Tip

Music at St Giles

St Giles Cathedral (p38) hosts many performances of classical and religious music. There are frequent lunchtime recitals, as well as the regular **St Giles at Six** series of concerts (every Sunday at 6pm); check the cathedral website for a detailed program.

Central Library. (www.thebongoclub.co.uk; 66 Cowgate; ☒2)

Cabaret Voltaire CLUB

32 ✪ Map p36, E3

An atmospheric warren of stone-lined vaults houses Edinburgh's most 'alternative' club, which eschews huge dance floors and egotistical DJ worship in favour of a 'creative crucible' hosting an eclectic mix of DJs, live acts, comedy, theatre, visual arts and spoken word. Well worth a look. (www.thecabaretvoltaire.com; 36-38 Blair St; ☒all South Bridge buses)

The Caves CLUB

33 ✪ Map p36, F3

A subterranean club venue set in the ancient stone vaults beneath the South Bridge, The Caves stages a series of infrequent but spectacular one-off club nights – check the What's On link on the website for upcoming events (☎557 8989; www.thecavesedinburgh.com; 8-12 Niddry St South; ☒35)

Bedlam Theatre COMEDY

34 ✪ Map p36, D4

The Bedlam hosts a long-established (more than 10 years) weekly improvisation slot, the Improverts, which is hugely popular with local students. Shows kick off at 10.30pm every Friday, and you're guaranteed a robust and entertaining evening. (☎225 9893; www.bedlamtheatre.co.uk; 11b Bristo Pl; admission £5; ☒2, 23, 27, 41, 42)

Local Life
Sandy Bell's

Sandy Bell's (Map p36, D5; 25 Forrest Rd) is an unassuming pub near the entrance to Greyfriars Kirkyard. It serves a good range of real ales and whiskies, but more importantly it's a stalwart of Edinburgh's traditional music scene (the founder's wife sang with famous 1970s folk group The Corries). There's live music almost every evening at 9pm, and from 3pm Saturday and Sunday, plus lots of impromptu sessions.

Jazz Bar   JAZZ

35 ⭐ Map p36, E4

This atmospheric cellar bar, with its polished parquet floors, bare stone walls, candlelit tables and stylish steel-framed chairs, is owned and operated by jazz musicians. There's live music every night from 9pm to 3am, and on Saturday from 3pm. (www.thejazzbar.co.uk; 1a Chambers St; admisson £3-4; 📶)

Liquid Room   CLUB, LIVE MUSIC

36 ⭐ Map p36, D3

Set in a subterranean vault deep beneath Victoria St, the Liquid Room is a superb club venue with a thundering sound system. There are regular club nights Wednesday to Saturday as well as live bands. (www.liquidroom.com; 9c Victoria St)

Edinburgh Folk Club   TRADITIONAL MUSIC

37 ⭐ Map p36, G4

The Pleasance Cabaret Bar is the home venue of the Edinburgh Folk Club, which runs a program of visiting bands and singers at 8pm on Wednesday nights; no need for membership, just buy your ticket at the door. The bar is a major Fringe venue, so there are no concerts here during the festival period. (www.edinburghfolkclub.co.uk; Pleasance Courtyard, 60 The Pleasance; admission £9; 🚌36)

Royal Oak   TRADITIONAL MUSIC

38 ⭐ Map p36, F4

This popular folk pub is tiny, so get there early (9pm start weekdays, 2.30pm Saturday) if you want to be sure of a place. Sunday from 4pm to 7pm is open session – bring your own instruments (or a good singing voice). (www.royal-oak-folk.com; 1 Infirmary St; 🚌all South Bridge buses)

Studio 24   CLUB

39 ⭐ Map p36, H1

Studio 24 is the dark heart of Edinburgh's underground music scene, with a program that covers all bases, from house to nu metal via punk, ska, reggae, crossover, tribal, electro, techno and dance. (www.studio24.me; 24 Calton Rd; 🚌35, 36)

Whistle Binkie's

LIVE MUSIC

40 ⭐ Map p36, E3

This crowded cellar bar, just off the Royal Mile, has live music every night till 3am, from rock and blues to folk and jazz. Open-mic night on Monday and breaking bands on Tuesday are showcases for new talent. Admission free, but cover charge for entry after midnight Friday and Saturday. (www. whistlebinkies.com; 4-6 South Bridge; 🚌all South Bridge buses)

Shopping

Armstrong's

FASHION

41 🔒 Map p36, C4

Armstrong's is an Edinburgh fashion institution (established in 1840, no less), a quality vintage clothes emporium offering everything from elegant 1940s dresses to funky 1970s flares. As well as having retro fashion, it's a great place to hunt for 'previously owned' kilts and Harris tweed, or to seek inspiration for that fancy-dress party. (📞220 5557; www.armstrongsvintage. co.uk; 83 Grassmarket; ⏰10am-5.30pm Mon-Thu, to 6pm Fri & Sat, noon-6pm Sun; 🚌2)

Vintage fashion inside Armstrong's

Avalanche Records
MUSIC

42 Map p36, B4

Avalanche is a sacred place of pilgrimage for music fans in search of good-value CDs, especially indie, rock and punk. (☎659 7708; www.avalancherecords.co.uk; 5 Grassmarket; ⏰11am-6pm Mon-Sat, noon-6pm Sun; 🚍2)

Local Life
Cockburn Street Shops

Cockburn St (Map p36, E2), curving down from the Royal Mile to Waverley train station, is the heart of Edinburgh's youth shopping scene, lined with quirky independent stores peddling everything from goth gear and body piercings to incense and healing crystals. Here you'll find one of the the city's best record shops, Underground Solush'n, as well as the following:

▶ **Cookie** (☎622 7260; 29 Cockburn St) Cute party dresses.

▶ **Liberation** (☎225 9831; 45 Cockburn St) T-shirts with slogans.

▶ **Route One** (☎226 2131; www.routeone.co.uk; 29 Cockburn St) Skate and BMX gear.

▶ **Whiplash Trash** (☎226 1005; 53 Cockburn St) Tattoos and body piercing.

Underground Solush'n
MUSIC

43 Map p36, D2

A paradise for searchers of new and secondhand vinyl, this place has thousands of records – techno, house, jungle, hip-hop, R&B, funk, soul and 45s – plus a (smaller) selection of CDs, T-shirts, videos, books and merchandise. It's also a good place to find out what's happening on the local music/clubbing scene. (☎226 2242; 9 Cockburn St; ⏰10am- 6pm Mon-Wed, Fri & Sat, 10am-7pm Thu, noon-6pm Sun; 🚍all South Bridge buses)

Royal Mile Whiskies
FOOD & DRINK

44 Map p36, D3

If it's a drap of the cratur ye're after, this place has a selection of single malts in miniature and full-size bottles. There's also a range of blended whiskies, Irish whiskey and bourbon, and you can buy online too. (☎225 3383; www.royalmilewhiskies.co.uk; 379 High St; ⏰10am-6pm Mon-Sat & 12.30-6pm Sun mid-Sep–Jun, 12.30-8pm daily Jul–mid-Sep; 🚍2, 23, 27, 41, 42)

Bill Baber
FASHION

45 Map p36, C4

This family-run designer knitwear studio has been in the business for more than 30 years, producing stylish and colourful creations using linen, merino wool, silk and cotton. (☎225 3249; www.billbaber.com; 66 Grassmarket; ⏰9am-5.30pm Mon-Sat; 🚍2)

Corniche
FASHION

46 Map p36, F2

A major stockist of designer clothes for women, with a selection of big-name labels such as Jean-Paul Gaultier, Vivienne Westwood, Anna Sui, Katharine Hamnett and Alexander McQueen. The branch next door concentrates on designer menswear. (556 3707; www.corniche.org.uk; 2 Jeffrey St; 10.30am-5.30pm Mon-Sat, 35)

Geoffrey (Tailor) Inc
FASHION

47 Map p36, F2

Can fit you out in traditional Highland dress, or run up a kilt in your own clan tartan. Its offshoot, 21st Century Kilts, offers modern fashion kilts in a variety of fabrics. (www.geoffreykilts.co.uk; 57-59 High St; 9.30am-5pm Mon-Sat, 11am-5pm Sun; 35)

Godiva
FASHION

48 Map p36, B4

This unconventional and innovative boutique specialising in both vintage and modern cutting-edge designs won Best New Designer prize in the Scottish Variety Awards 2010. (22. 9212; www.godivaboutique.co.uk, 9 West Port; 10am-6pm Mon-Sat, 11.30am-5pm Sun; 2)

Joyce Forsyth Designer Knitwear
FASHION

49 Map p36, D4

Colourful designs that will drag your ideas about woollens firmly into the 21st century. (220 4112; www.joyceforsyth.co.uk; 42 Candlemaker Row; 10am-5.30pm Tue-Sat)

Mr Wood's Fossils
GIFTS

50 Map p36, C4

Founded by the famous fossil hunter who discovered 'Lizzie', the oldest fossil reptile yet discovered, this fascinating speciality shop has a wide range of minerals, gems, fossils and other geological gifts. (220 1344; www.mrwoodsfossils.co.uk; 5 Cowgatehead; 10am-5.30pm Mon-Sat; 2)

Explore

Holyrood & Arthur's Seat

Facing the imposing royal palace of Holyroodhouse at the foot of the Royal Mile, a once near-derelict district has been transformed by the construction of the Scottish Parliament Building. Holyrood Park, a former hunting ground of Scottish monarchs centred on the miniature mountain of Arthur's Seat, allows Edinburghers to enjoy a little bit of wilderness in the heart of the city.

The Sights in a Day

🔅 Spend the best part of the morning taking a self-guided tour of the **Palace of Holyroodhouse** (p56) before breaking for lunch in the **Café at the Palace** (p57), or at **Hemma** (p65).

☀️ If the weather is good, devote the afternoon to exploring Holyrood Park, climbing to the top of **Arthur's Seat** (p63) for a fantastic view of the city and the Firth of Forth. If it's too cold or wet for outdoor exploration, take a tour of the **Scottish Parliament Building** (p58) followed by a visit to **Our Dynamic Earth** (p63).

🌙 In summer, you could do worse than end your day at the **Sheep Heid Inn** (p61) for a pub dinner in the beer garden. In winter book a table at **Rhubarb** (p64) and dress up for an evening of divine decadence.

For a local's day in Holyrood & Arthur's Seat, see p60.

👁 Top Sights

Palace of Holyroodhouse (p56)
Scottish Parliament Building (p58)

○ Local Life

A Walk Through Holyrood Park (p60)

♥ Best of Edinburgh

Views
Arthur's Seat (p63)

Architecture
Scottish Parliament Building (p58)

For Kids
Our Dynamic Earth (p63)

Drinking
Sheep Heid Inn (p61)

Getting There

🚌 **Bus** Lothian Buses 35 and 36 both run to Holyrood, 35 via the lower half of the Royal Mile and 36 via Holyrood Rd. Bus 42 runs along Duddingston Rd West, a short walk from Duddingston Village, while 4, 5, 15, 26, 44 and 45 run along London Rd, near the north entrance to Holyrood Park.

Top Sights
Palace of Holyroodhouse

This palace is the royal family's official residence in Scotland, serving as a home from home when the queen is visiting Edinburgh. But it is probably more famous as the 16th-century home of the ill-fated Mary, Queen of Scots, who spent six turbulent years here (1561–67), during which time she debated with John Knox, married both her first and second husbands, and witnessed the murder of her secretary (and rumoured lover) David Rizzio.

Map p62, B1

www.royalcollection.org.uk

Horse Wynd

adult/child £11/6.65

9.30am-6pm Apr-Oct, to 4.30pm Nov-Mar

Holyrood Abbey

Don't Miss

Great Gallery

The self-guided audio tour leads you through a series of impressive royal apartments, ending in the Great Gallery. The 89 portraits of Scottish kings (both real and legendary) were commissioned by Charles II and supposedly record his unbroken lineage from Scota, the Egyptian pharaoh's daughter who discovered the infant Moses in a reed basket on the banks of the Nile.

Mary's Bedchamber

The highlight of the tour is the bedchamber of Mary, Queen of Scots, home to the unfortunate Mary from 1561 to 1567 (it's connected to her husband's bedchamber by a secret stairway). It was here that her jealous first husband, Lord Darnley, restrained the pregnant queen while his henchmen murdered her secretary – and favourite – David Rizzio; a plaque in the neighbouring room marks the spot where he bled to death.

Holyrood Abbey

Admission to the palace includes a guided tour of neighbouring Holyrood Abbey (April to October only), founded by King David I in 1128. It was probably named after a fragment of the True Cross, on which Christ was crucified (rood is an old Scots word for cross), said to have been brought back from the Holy Land by his mother, St Margaret. Most of the surviving ruins date from the 12th and 13th centuries; the royal burial vault holds the remains of kings David II, James II and James V, and of Lord Darnley, husband of Mary, Queen of Scots.

☑ Top Tips

► The palace is closed to the public when the royal family is visiting and during state functions (usually in mid-May, and mid-June to early July); check the website for exact dates.

► You can wander through the palace at your own speed; an audioguide is included in the price of admission. Allow at least one to 1½ hours.

► If you plan to visit the Queen's Gallery (p64) too, you can buy a combined ticket (£15.50/8.80 per adult/child).

✕ Take a Break

The **Café at the Palace** (Mews Courtyard, Queen's Gallery; mains £6-10; ⊙9.30am-6pm Apr-Oct, to 4.30pm Nov-Mar), in the courtyard of the Queen's Gallery, serves soup and snacks, including baked potato with haggis. Foodies at Holyrood (p64) is a short walk away.

Top Sights
Scottish Parliament Building

The Scottish Parliament Building is a spectacular example of modern architecture, designed by Catalan architect Enric Miralles and officially opened by the queen in 2005. It's an original and idiosyncratic building that caused a great deal of controversy at the time, and now provides a home for the new parliament that was created in the wake of the Scottish devolution referendum of 1997 (the previous Scottish parliament had been dissolved following the Act of Union in 1707).

Map p62, A1

www.scottish.
parliament.uk

Horse Wynd

admission free

9am-6.30pm Tue-Thu, 10am-5.30pm Mon, Fri & Sat in session, 10am-6pm Mon-Sat in recess

Debating Chamber

Don't Miss

The Exterior

The architect Enric Miralles (1955–2000) believed that a building could be a work of art. However, this weird concrete confection has left many people scratching their heads in confusion. What does it all mean? The strange forms of the exterior are all symbolic in some way, from the oddly shaped **projecting windows** on the west wall (inspired by the silhouette of *Reverend Robert Walker Skating on Duddingston Loch*, one of Scotland's most famous paintings), to the unusual, inverted-L-shaped **panels** on the facade (representing a curtain being drawn aside, ie open government). Even the ground plan of the whole complex represents a 'flower of democracy rooted in Scottish soil' (best seen looking down from Salisbury Crags).

The Debating Chamber

The **Main Hall**, inside the public entrance, has a low, triple-arched ceiling of polished concrete, like a cave, or cellar, or castle vault. It is a dimly lit space, the starting point for a metaphorical journey from this relative darkness up to the **Debating Chamber** (sitting directly above the Main Hall), which is, in contrast, a palace of light – the light of democracy. This magnificent chamber is the centrepiece of the parliament, designed not to glorify but to humble the politicians who sit within it. The windows face Calton Hill, allowing Members of Scottish Parliament (MSPs) to look up to its monuments (reminders of the Scottish Enlightenment), while the massive, pointed oak beams of the roof are suspended by steel threads above the MSPs' heads like so many Damoclean swords.

☑ Top Tips

▶ The public areas of the Parliament Building – the Main Hall, where there is an exhibition, a shop and cafe, and the public gallery in the Debating Chamber – are open to visitors (tickets needed for public gallery – see website for details).

▶ You can also take a free, one-hour guided tour (advance booking recommended).

▶ If you want to see the parliament in session, check the website for sitting times – business days are normally Tuesday to Thursday year-round.

✗ Take a Break

There is a cafe in the Parliament Building at the rear of the Main Hall, and another across the street in the Queen's Gallery. Alternatively, Foodies at Holyrood (p64) is just around the corner.

Local Life
A Walk Through Holyrood Park

Holyrood Park covers 650 acres of varied landscape, including crags, moorland and lochs, plus the miniature mountain of Arthur's Seat, little changed since its enclosure as a royal hunting ground in the 16th century. It's a wildlife haven and a huge recreational resource for the city, thronged with walkers, cyclists and picnickers on sunny weekends.

1 St Margaret's Loch
Begin at the park's northern entrance on Duke's Walk, which leads to St Margaret's Loch, an artificial pond created during Victorian times. The loch is well known for its huge flocks of swans and ducks (please don't feed them – human food is not healthy for wild animals).

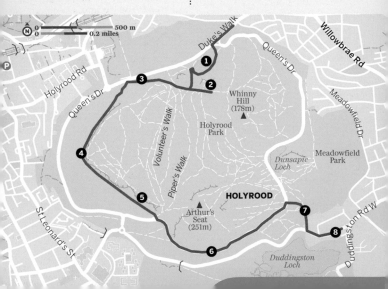

❷ St Anthony's Chapel

Take the path on the south side of the loch and climb up to the ruins of St Anthony's Chapel. Dating from the 15th century, its origins are obscure; it may have been associated with a hospital in Leith donated by King James I (for the treatment of the skin disease erysipelas, also known as St Anthony's Fire), or it may have been a beacon for ships in the Firth of Forth.

❸ St Margaret's Well

Descend back to the road where you'll find St Margaret's Well, a beautiful, late-15th-century Gothic well-house. It was moved, stone by stone, to this location in 1860 when its original site in Meadowbank was taken over by a railway depot. You can't get into the chamber – all you can do is peek at the ornate vaulting through the metal grille at the entrance.

❹ Radical Road

The park's most dramatic feature is the long, curving sweep of Salisbury Crags, a russet curtain of columnar basaltic cliffs. The stony path along the foot of the crags is known as the Radical Road – it was built in 1820 at the suggestion of Sir Walter Scott, to give work to unemployed weavers (from whose politics it took its name).

❺ Hutton's Section

At the southern end of the crags, look out for an interpretation board set in a boulder marking Hutton's Section. Edinburgh's most famous rock outcrop was used by the pioneering geologist James Hutton in 1788 to bolster his theory that the basaltic rocks of Salisbury Crags were formed by the cooling of molten lava.

❻ Queen's Drive

Continue onto Queen's Dr, built in the 19th century as a scenic carriage drive for Queen Victoria and Prince Albert during their stays at Holyroodhouse. Closed to motor vehicles on Sundays, the drive winds across the southern slopes of Arthur's Seat, with grand views over the city to the Pentland Hills.

❼ Jacob's Ladder

Where the road curves sharply to the north (left), a footpath on the right (signposted) leads to Jacob's Ladder, a steep staircase of 209 steps that descends to the western edge of Duddingston Village.

❽ Duddingston Village

The picturesque little village of Duddingston dates from the 12th century, though only the church survives from that era; most of the houses are 18th-century, including the village pub, the Sheep Heid Inn (p65), a good place to stop for lunch or a pint. Nearby is **Prince Charlie's Cottage**, where the Young Pretender held a council of war before the Battle of Prestonpans in 1745.

Calton
New Burial
Ground

Abbeyhill

Queen's
Gallery

⊙ 4

**Palace of
Holyroodhouse**

Canongate
(Royal Mile)

Horse
Wynd

Reid's
Cl

**Scottish
Parliament
Building**

Queen's Dr

Holyrood Rd

6 7

1 ⊙
Our Dynamic
Earth

Queen's Dr

Queen's Dr

N 0 ———— 200 m
   0 ———— 0.1 miles

Duke's Walk

St Margaret's
Loch

Holyrood
Park

Volunteer's Walk

Piper's Walk

Radical Road

For reviews see

◉ Top Sights	p56
⊙ Sights	p63
✕ Eating	p64
⊖ Drinking	p65

Arthur's
Seat ⊙2
Arthur's
Seat
(251m)

Dalkeith Rd

Holyrood Park Rd

University of
Edinburgh
Pollock Halls
of Residence

Prestonfield
Golf Course

Queen's Dr

8 ⊖

5
✕

3 ⊙

Sights

Our Dynamic Earth EXHIBITION

1 ◉ Map p62, A2

A white marquee pitched beneath Salisbury Crags marks this interactive, multimedia journey of discovery through the earth's history from the Big Bang to the present day. Hugely popular with kids of all ages, it's a slick extravaganza of whiz-bang special effects and 3D movies cleverly designed to fire up young minds with curiosity about all things geological and environmental. (www.dynamicearth. co.uk; Holyrood Rd; adult/child £11.50/7.50; ⊙10am-6pm daily Jul & Aug, to 5.30pm Apr–Jun, Sep & Oct, 10am-5pm Wed-Sun Nov-Mar, last admission 90min before closing; 🚻; 🚌35, 36)

Arthur's Seat LANDMARK

2 ◉ Map p62, D4

The rocky peak of Arthur's Seat (251m), carved by ice sheets from the deeply eroded stump of a long-extinct volcano, is a distinctive feature of Edinburgh's skyline. The view from the summit is worth the hike, extending from the Forth Bridges in the west to the distant conical hill of North Berwick Law in the east, with the Ochil Hills and the Highlands on the northwestern horizon. (Holyrood Park)

Duddingston Parish Church CHURCH

3 ◉ Map p62, D5

This medieval church is one of the oldest buildings in Edinburgh, with a 12th-century Romanesque doorway and some interesting medieval relics at the kirkyard gate: the Joug, a metal collar that was used, like the stocks, to tether criminals and sinners, and the Loupin-On Stane, a stone step to help gouty and corpulent parishioners get onto their horses. (www.duddingstonkirk.co.uk; Old Church Lane; ⊙church 1-4pm Thu & 2-4pm Sun Aug only, kirkyard dawn–dusk; 🚌42)

Our Dynamic Earth

ANDY S'OTHERT/GETTY IMAGES ©

Understand
Mystery of the Miniature Coffins

In July 1836 five boys hunting for rabbits on the slopes of Arthur's Seat made a strange discovery: in a hollow beneath a rock, arranged on a pile of slates, were 17 tiny wooden coffins. Each was just 4 inches (10cm) long and contained a roughly carved human figure dressed in handmade clothes.

Many theories have been put forward in explanation, but the most convincing is that the coffins were made in response to the infamous Burke and Hare murders of 1831–32: the number of coffins matched the number of known victims. It was a common belief that people whose bodies had been dissected by anatomists could not enter heaven, and it is thought that someone fashioned the tiny figures in order to provide the murder victims with a form of Christian burial.

Eight of the 17 coffins survive, and can be seen in the National Museum of Scotland (p32). Edinburgh author Ian Rankin makes use of the story of the coffins in his detective novel *The Falls*.

Queen's Gallery

GALLERY

4 🎯 Map p62, B1

This stunning modern gallery, which occupies the shell of a former church and school, is a showcase for exhibitions of art from the Royal Collections. The exhibitions change every six months or so; for details of the latest, check the website. (www.royalcollection.org.uk; Horse Wynd; adult/child £6.25/3.15, joint ticket incl admission to palace £15.50/8.80; ⏱9.30am-6pm Apr-Oct, to 4.30pm Nov-Mar; 🚌35, 36)

Eating

Rhubarb

SCOTTISH £££

5 🍴 Map p62, A5

Set in the splendid 17th-century Prestonfield House, Rhubarb is a feast for the eyes as well as the taste buds; the over-the-top decor and the sensuous surfaces – damask, brocade, marble, gilded leather – are matched by the intense flavours and rich textures of the food. Set menus include a two-course lunch for £17, and three-course lunch or dinner for £33. (📞225 1333; Prestonfield House Hotel, Priestfield Rd; mains £26-35; ⏱lunch & dinner)

Foodies at Holyrood

CAFE £

6 🍴 Map p62, A2

This stylish cafe, handy for a post-sightseeing snack after visiting Holyroodhouse or Our Dynamic Earth, is dedicated to serving top-quality, locally sourced produce. Healthy breakfasts range from homemade muesli to porridge with apple, sultanas and cinnamon, while the

Urban Hillwalking on Arthur's Seat

To climb Arthur's Seat from Holyrood, cross Queen's Dr and follow the path that slants leftwards up the hillside from the north end of Salisbury Crags, heading towards the ruins of St Anthony's Chapel, then turn south on a rough path that follows the floor of a shallow dip just east of Long Row crags. The path eventually curves around to the left and rises more steeply up some steps to a saddle; turn right here and climb to the rocky summit of Arthur's Seat.

lunch menu includes soups, freshly prepared sandwiches, ciabattas and baked potatoes. (☏557 6836; www.foodiesatholyrood.com; G7 Holyrood Rd; mains £4-7; ⊙8am-6pm Mon-Fri, 10am-6pm Sat & Sun; 🛜♿; 🚌36)

Drinking

Hemma   BAR

7 📍 Map p62, A2

Set among the glass-and-steel architecture of the redeveloped Holyrood district, Hemma (Swedish for 'at home') is the latest in a line of Scandinavian bars, a funky fish-tank of a place furnished with comfy armchairs and sofas and brightly coloured wooden chairs. Good coffee and cakes during the day, real ale and cocktails in the evening. (☏629 3327; www.boda bar.com; 75 Holyrood Rd; 🛜♿; 🚌36)

Sheep Heid Inn   PUB

8 📍 Map p62, D5

Possibly the oldest inn in Edinburgh (with a licence dating back to 1360), the Sheep Heid feels more like a country pub than an Edinburgh bar. Set in the semirural shadow of Arthur's Seat, it's famous for its 19th-century skittles alley and lovely little beer garden. (www.thesheepheidedinburgh.co.uk; 43-45 The Causeway; ♿; 🚌42)

Explore

New Town

Edinburgh's New Town is the world's most complete and unspoilt example of Georgian architecture and town planning; along with the Old Town, it was declared a Unesco World Heritage Site in 1995. Princes St is one of Britain's most spectacular shopping streets, with unbroken views of the castle, while George St is lined with designer boutiques, trendy bars and upmarket restaurants.

The Sights in a Day

☀ Begin the day with a stroll through the western part of **Princes Street Gardens**, and plan on spending the rest of the morning admiring the art at the **Scottish National Gallery** (p76) and the **Royal Scottish Academy** (p76) before enjoying a Scottish-themed lunch at the gallery's **Scottish Cafe & Restaurant** (p71).

☼ Continue through the eastern part of the gardens, or along Princes St, to St Andrew Sq and another bout of art appreciation at the **Scottish National Portrait Gallery** (p68). Browse the boutiques in nearby Multrees Walk, or explore the independent shops along George St, Thistle St and Rose St, before climbing **Calton Hill** (p77) for a magnificent sunset view.

☾ Relax with a cocktail at **Bramble** (p84) before getting a taxi to **Gardener's Cottage** (p81) or **21212** (p83) for an unforgettable dinner (be sure to book in advance), then catch some live jazz at the **Jam House** (p86) or a comedy act at **The Stand** (p86).

For a local's day in the New Town, see p72.

👁 Top Sights

Scottish National Portrait Gallery (p68)

Princes Street Gardens (p70)

🔍 Local Life

New Town Shopping (p72)

♥ Best of Edinburgh

Shopping
Jenners (p72)
Harvey Nichols (p73)
Alchemia (p73)

Eating
Gardener's Cottage (p81)
The Dogs (p81)
Scottish Cafe & Restaurant (p71)

Drinking
Café Royal Circle Bar (p84)
Bramble (p84)
Guildford Arms (p84)
Amicus Apple (p85)

Getting There

🚌 **Bus** Just about every bus service in Edinburgh runs along Princes St at some point in its journey. But note that not all buses stop at every bus stop – if you're looking for a particular bus, check the route numbers listed on the bus-stop sign.

Top Sights
Scottish National Portrait Gallery

The Venetian Gothic palace of the Scottish National Portrait Gallery reopened its doors in 2011 after a two-year renovation, emerging as one of the city's top attractions. Its galleries illustrate Scottish history through paintings, photographs and sculptures, putting faces to famous names from Scotland's past and present, from Robert Burns, Mary, Queen of Scots and Bonnie Prince Charlie to actor Sean Connery, comedian Billy Connolly and poet Jackie Kay.

👁 Map p74, D3

www.nationalgalleries.org

1 Queen St

admission free

🕙10am-5pm Fri-Wed, to 7pm Thu

Great Hall

Don't Miss

Architecture

The museum's exterior is a neo-Gothic froth of friezes, pinnacles and sculptures – the niches at 1st-floor level hold statues of Scottish kings and queens, philosophers and poets, artists and scientists. Mary, Queen of Scots is in the middle of the east wall on North St Andrew St, while the main entrance is framed by Robert the Bruce and William Wallace.

Great Hall

The gallery's interior is decorated in Arts and Crafts style, nowhere more splendidly than in the Great Hall. Above the Gothic colonnade a processional frieze painted by William Hole in 1898 serves as a 'visual encyclopedia' of famous Scots, shown in chronological order from Calgacus (the chieftain who led the Caledonian tribes into battle against the Romans) to writer and philosopher Thomas Carlyle (1795–1881). The murals on the 1st-floor balcony depict scenes from Scottish history, while the ceiling is painted with the constellations of the night sky.

Bonnie Prince Charlie

Contrast the 1750 portrait of a dashing Prince Charles Edward Stuart (1720–88), in tartan suit and Jacobite bonnet, at a time when he still had hopes of returning to Scotland to claim the throne, and the one painted towards the end of his life – exiled in Rome, an alcoholic, a broken man.

Three Oncologists (2002)

This eerie portrait by Ken Currie, of three leading cancer specialists, somehow captures the horror of the disease along with the sense that their achievements in treating it are a kind of alchemical mystery.

☑ **Top Tips**

▶ The gallery's selection of 'trails' leaflets adds a bit of background information while leading you around the various exhibits; the Hidden Histories trail is particularly interesting.

▶ Free guided tours of the gallery's architecture are held at 2pm on the third Saturday of the month – best to book in advance on ☎624 6560.

✕ **Take a Break**

The excellent soups and sandwiches at the gallery's **Cafe Portrait** (mains £6-8; ⊙10am-4.30pm Fri-Wed, to 6pm Thu; 🛜) make it a popular lunch spot for local office workers. If it's too crowded here, head a block west to The Dogs (p81) for top nosh at great-value prices.

Top Sights
Princes Street Gardens

These beautiful gardens are slung between Edinburgh's Old and New Towns, occupying a valley that once held the Nor' Loch, a boggy depression that was drained in the early 19th century. The gardens are split in the middle by the Mound – around two million cart-loads of earth were dug out from foundations during the construction of the New Town and dumped here to provide a road link across the valley to the Old Town. It was completed in 1830.

◉ Map p74, B5

Princes St

admission free

⊙ dawn-dusk

🚌 all Princes St buses

Don't Miss

Scott Monument

The eastern half of Princes Street Gardens is dominated by the massive Gothic spire of the **Scott Monument** (www.edinburghmuseums.org.uk; admission £3; ⏰10am-7pm Mon-Sat Apr-Sep, 9am-4pm Mon-Sat Oct-Mar, 10am-6pm Sun year-round), built by public subscription in memory of the novelist Sir Walter Scott after his death in 1832. The exterior is decorated with carvings of characters from his novels; inside you can see an exhibition on Scott's life, and climb the 287 steps to the top for a superb view of the city.

West End Churches

The western end of the gardens is dominated by the tower of **St John's Church**, worth visiting for its fine Gothic Revival interior. It overlooks **St Cuthbert's Parish Church**, built in the 1890s on a site of great antiquity – there has been a church here since at least the 12th century, and perhaps since the 7th century. There is a circular **Watch Tower** in the graveyard, a reminder of the days when graves had to be guarded against bodysnatchers.

Floral Clock & Ross Bandstand

At the entrance to the western gardens on the corner of Princes St and the Mound is the **Floral Clock**, a working clock laid out in flowers; it was first created in 1903 and the design changes every year. In the middle of the western part of the gardens is the **Ross Bandstand**, a venue for open-air concerts in summer and at Hogmanay, and the stage for the famous Fireworks Concert during the Edinburgh Festival.

☑ Top Tips

▶ The gardens are home to events throughout the year, from the Edinburgh Festival Fireworks Concert to the Christmas Market and ice-skating rink in December. See www.edinburghfestivals.co.uk/venues/princes-street-gardens.

▶ Spring is the time to see the gardens' flower displays at their best – in April the slopes below the castle esplanade are thick with yellow daffodils.

▶ On Saturday you can buy food from the farmers market on Castle Terrace, then grab a bench in the neighbouring gardens for an al fresco meal.

✖ Take a Break

The **Scottish Cafe & Restaurant** (☎226 6524; www.thescottishcafeandrestaurant.com; The Mound; mains £10-16; ⏰9am-5pm Mon-Wed, Fri & Sat, to 7pm Thu, 10am-5pm Sun; 🛜), beneath the Royal Scottish Academy, offers traditional Scottish cuisine with a garden view.

Local Life
New Town Shopping

Shopping in the New Town offers everything from mall-crawling and traditional department stores to browsing in dinky little designer boutiques and rubbing shoulder-bags with fussing fashionistas in Harvey Nicks. And all in a compact city centre that you can cover without blowing the bank on taxis or getting blisters from your Blahniks.

❶ Jenners

Founded in 1838, **Jenners** (www.houseoffraser.co.uk; 48 Princes St; 🚍 all Princes St buses) is the grande dame of Edinburgh shopping. Its five floors stock a wide range of quality goods, both classic and contemporary (it's especially strong on designer shoes and handbags, hats, knitwear and oriental rugs) plus food hall, hairdresser, gift-wrapping service and four cafes.

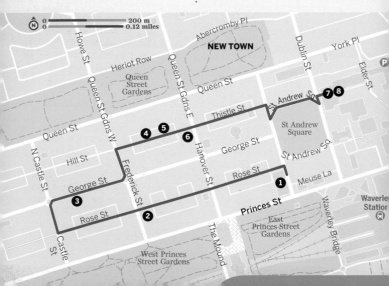

❷ Rose Street

Pedestrianised Rose St was once notorious as a pub crawl; there are still pubs, but the street is better known today for shops, mostly mainstream, which range from outdoor sports emporiums such as Cotswold Outdoor and Tiso to antique jewellery specialists like **Alistir Wood Tait** (www.alistirtait gem.co.uk; 116a Rose St; ⊙Tue-Sat; 🚍all Princes St buses).

❸ Cruise

An ornately corniced foyer leads into three floors of minimalist gallery-like decor. This **branch** (☎226 3524; www. cruisefashion.co.uk; 94 George St; ⊙10am-6pm Mon-Fri, 9.30am-6pm Sat, noon-5pm Sun; 🚍19, 37, 41) and an outlet at nearby 80 George St show off the best of mainstream designer labels including Paul Smith, Jasper Conran, Hugo Boss, Joseph Tricot, Armani and Dolce & Gabbana.

❹ Kakao by K

Thistle St, Rose St's partner to the north of George St, has become an enclave of designer boutiques. **Kakao by K** (☎226 3584; www.kakao.co.uk; 45 Thistle St; ⊙Mon-Sat; 🚍23, 27) is typical, a showcase for Scandinavian fashion labels such as Fillipa K and House of Lykke, as well as handbags, scarves and even jewellery designed by the shop's Danish owner.

❺ Alchemia

Made in a workshop in Fife, the jewellery on display at **Alchemia**

(☎220 4795; www.alchemia.co.uk; 37 Thistle St; ⊙Tue-Sat; 🚍23, 27) is designed in Scotland and inspired by the shapes and colours of the natural world. If nothing catches your eye, you can request bespoke jewellery – former clients have included royalty.

❻ Covet

Another Thistle St stalwart, **Covet** (☎220 0026; thoushaltcovet.com; 20 Thistle St; ⊙Mon-Sat; 🚍23, 27) has an emphasis on up-and-coming new designers from all over the world. Look for bags by Dutch label Smaak and New York designer Rebecca Minkoff, jewellery by Tatty Devine, and watches from Swedish brand Triwa.

❼ Harvey Nichols

The jewel in the crown of Edinburgh's shopping scene, **Harvey Nichols** (www. harveynichols.com; 30-34 St Andrew Sq; 🚍all St Andrew Sq buses) has four floors of designer labels and is the anchor for the Multrees Walk luxury shopping mall. Nearby you'll find boutiques by Louis Vuitton, Mulberry, Hugo Boss, Swarovski and more.

❽ Valvona & Crolla VinCaffè

By now you'll be looking forward to a break; **VinCaffè** (☎557 0088; www. valvonacrolla.co.uk; 11 Multrees Walk, St Andrew Sq; mains £10-17; ⊙8am-11pm Mon-Sat, noon-5pm Sun; 🛜; 🚍all St Andrew Sq buses) is an ideal place for lunch, or perhaps just a bottle of pinot grigio shared over a platter of antipasti.

STOCKBRIDGE

A

Edinburgh
Academy

B

Eyre Pl

C

King
George V
Park

D

Dean Bank La

Hamilton Pl

Henderson Row

W Silvermills La

Clarence St

Fettes Row

Royal Cres

Scotland St

1

Cumberland St

Dundonald St

25

Drummond Pl

Kerr St

St Stephen St

Circus La

St Vincent St

Great King St

2

NW Circus Pl

Circus Pl

Howe St

Dundas St

Northumberland St

Dublin St

India Pl

Circus Pl

Royal Circus

39 🔒

Dean
Gardens

Gloucester La

India St

28 🔒

Jamaica Mews

Abercromby Pl

**Scottish Nationa
Portrait Gallery**

◉

Moray Pl

Heriot Row

Queen Street
Gardens

Queen St Gdns E

Queen St

31 ✪

3

Queen St Gdns W

14 ✕ ✕ 18

St Colme
St

Thistle St

21 🔒

Hill St

15 ✕

19 ✕

33 ✪

George St

44 🔒

3 ◉
*Georgian
House*

Young St

26 🔒

N Castle St

38 43 45
🔒 🔒 🔒

Frederick St

Hanover St

Rose St

4

30 🔒

George St

46 🔒

27 🔒

Castle St

*Royal
Scottish
Academy*

2 ◉

4 *Charlotte
Square* ◉

Charlotte
Square

S Charlotte St

Rose St

Princes St

East Princes
Street
Gardens

Hope St

**Princes
Street
Gardens** ◉

West Princes
Street
Gardens

1 ◉

*Scottish Nationa
Gallery*

N Bank St

37 🔒

5

29
Bellevue
Bellevue Cres

Mansfield 11
Place Church

E London St

13

17

NEW
TOWN

Gayfield St

Gayfield St

Gayfield Sq

Leith Walk

Brunswick St

40

23
41

Windsor St

16
Barony St
Albany St La

Broughton Pl

Edinburgh
Printmakers'
Workshop 10
& Gallery

Union St

London Rd

12

Albany St

York La

Forth St

Broughton St La

Broughton St

35

36

Royal Terrace
Gardens
Royal Tce

20

York Pl

Cathedral La

Regent
Gardens

32

Edinburgh
Bus Station &
First Edinburgh
Bus Shop 42

Elder St

P

St James
Shopping
Centre

Omni
Centre

Greenside Row

P

Calton
Hill

5

City
Observatory

National
7 Monument

Regent Gardens

St Andrew
Square

34 22

24

Leith St

Waterloo Pl

8

Old Calton
Burial
Ground

North Bridge

St Andrew's
House

Calton Rd

6
Nelson
Monument

Calton
Hill

Royal High
School

Regent Rd

Burns
Monument 9

Waverley
Station

Waverley Bridge

P

E Market St

P

New St

Canongate
Kirk

Canongate (Royal Mile)

Market St

High St (Royal Mile)

St Mary's
St

OLD
TOWN

St John St

For reviews see

Sights

Scottish National Gallery

GALLERY

1 ◉ Map p74, D5

Scotland's premier collection of art is housed in this imposing neoclassical building. The galleries dedicated to Scottish art include glowing portraits by Allan Ramsay and Sir Henry Raeburn, rural scenes by Sir David Wilkie and impressionistic landscapes by William MacTaggart. Look out for Raeburn's iconic *Reverend Robert Walker Skating on Duddingston Loch*. Once a year, in January, the gallery exhibits its collection of Turner watercolours, bequeathed by Henry Vaughan in 1900. (☏624 6200; www.nationalgalleries.org; The Mound; admission free, fee for special exhibitions; ◷10am-5pm Fri-Wed, to 7pm Thu, noon-5pm 1 Jan, closed 25 & 26 Dec; ▣all Princes St buses)

Royal Scottish Academy

GALLERY

2 ◉ Map p74, D4

The distinguished Greek Doric temple was designed by William Playfair and built between 1823 and 1836. The galleries display a collection of paintings, sculptures and architectural drawings by academy members dating from 1831, and also host temporary exhibitions throughout the year. The RSA and the Scottish National Gallery are linked via an underground mall – the Weston Link. (www.royalscottishacademy.org; The Mound; fee for special exhibitions; ◷10am-5pm Mon-Sat, 2-5pm Sun; ▣all Princes St buses)

Georgian House

HISTORIC BUILDING

3 ◉ Map p74, A4

The National Trust for Scotland's Georgian House has been beautifully restored and furnished to show how Edinburgh's wealthy elite lived at the end of the 18th century. The walls are decorated with paintings by Allan Ramsay, Sir Henry Raeburn and Sir Joshua Reynolds. (NTS; 7 Charlotte Sq; adult/child £6.50/5; ◷10am-6pm Jul & Aug, to 5pm Apr-Jun & Sep-Oct, 11am-4pm Mar, to 3pm Nov; ▣19, 36, 37, 41, 47)

Charlotte Square

SQUARE

4 ◉ Map p74, A4

Charlotte Sq is the architectural jewel of the New Town, designed by Robert Adam shortly before his death in 1791. The northern side of the square is Adam's masterpiece and one of the finest examples of Georgian architecture anywhere. Bute House, in the centre at No 6, is the official residence of Scotland's first minister. (▣19, 36, 37, 41, 47)

☑ Top Tip

Bus Info on Your Phone

Lothian Buses has created free smartphone apps that provide route maps, timetables and live waiting times for city buses. Search for EdinBus (iPhone), My Bus Edinburgh (Android) or Bus Tracker Edinburgh (Windows Phone).

Understand
New Town History

Between the end of the 14th century and the start of the 18th, the population of Edinburgh – still confined within the walls of the Old Town – increased from 2000 to 50,000. The tottering tenements were unsafe and occasionally collapsed, fire was an ever-present danger and the overcrowding and squalor became unbearable. There was no sewer system and household waste was disposed of by flinging it from the window into the street with a euphemistic shout of 'Gardyloo!' (from the French 'gardez l'eau' – beware of the water). Passersby replied with 'Haud yer haun'!' (Hold your hand) but were often too late. The stink that rose from the streets was ironically referred to as 'the floo'rs o' Edinburgh' (the flowers of Edinburgh).

So when the Act of Union in 1707 brought the prospect of long-term stability, the upper classes wanted healthier, more spacious living quarters, and in 1766 the Lord Provost of Edinburgh announced a competition to design an extension to the city. It was won by an unknown 23-year old, James Craig, a self-taught architect whose elegant plan envisaged the New Town's main axis, George St, following the crest of a ridge to the north of the Old Town, with grand squares at each end. Building was restricted to just one side of Princes St and Queen St, so that the houses had views over the Firth of Forth to the north, and to the castle and Old Town to the south.

During the 18th and 19th centuries, the New Town continued to sprout squares, circuses, parks and terraces, with some of its finest neoclassical architecture designed by Robert Adam. Today it is one of the world's finest examples of a Georgian cityscape, and is part of a Unesco World Heritage Site.

Calton Hill   VIEWPOINT

5 ⊙ Map p74, G3

Calton Hill, which rises dramatically above the eastern end of Princes St, is Edinburgh's acropolis, its summit scattered with grandiose monuments dating mostly from the first half of the 19th century. It is also one of the best viewpoints in Edinburgh, with a panorama that takes in the castle, Holyrood, Arthur's Seat, the Firth of Forth, New Town and the full length of Princes St.

On Regent Rd, on the hill's southern side, is the Burns Monument (p79), a Greek-style memorial to poet Robert Burns. (🚌 all Princes St buses)

Nelson Monument   MONUMENT

6 ⊙ Map p74, G3

Looking a bit like an upturned telescope – the similarity is intentional – and offering even better views, the

> ## Understand
> ## Hotbed of Genius
>
> Although Edinburgh declined in political importance following the Act of Union in 1707, its cultural and intellectual life flourished. During the period now called the Scottish Enlightenment (roughly 1740–1830), Edinburgh became known as 'a hotbed of genius', famed throughout Europe for its great philosophers, scientists and artists. In 1762 no less a figure than Voltaire declared that 'today it is from Scotland that we get rules of taste in all the arts, from epic poetry to gardening'.
>
> Enlightenment Edinburgh was home to philosopher David Hume, author of the influential *Treatise On Human Nature,* and political economist Adam Smith, who wrote *The Wealth of Nations*. Medic William Cullen produced the first modern pharmacopoeia, chemist Joseph Black advanced the science of thermodynamics, and geologist James Hutton challenged long-held beliefs about the age of the earth. Publisher William Smellie established the Encyclopaedia Britannica, and architect Robert Adam emerged as Britain's greatest exponent of neoclassicism.

Nelson Monument was built to commemorate Admiral Lord Nelson's victory at Trafalgar in 1805. (www.edinburghmuseums.org.uk; Calton Hill; admission £4; ◷10am-7pm Mon-Sat & noon-5pm Sun Apr-Sep, 10am-3pm Mon-Sat Oct-Mar; 🚌all Leith St buses)

National Monument   MONUMENT

7 ◉ Map p74, G3

The largest structure on the summit of Calton Hill, the National Monument was a rather over-ambitious attempt to replicate the Parthenon, and was intended to honour Scotland's dead in the Napoleonic Wars. Construction (paid for by public subscription) began in 1822 but funds ran dry when only 12 columns had been

erected. It became known locally as 'Edinburgh's Disgrace'. (Calton Hill)

Old Calton
Burial Ground   CEMETERY

8 ◉ Map p74, F4

One of Edinburgh's many atmospheric old cemeteries, Old Calton is a peaceful retreat just a short stroll from the east end of Princes St. It's dominated by the tall black obelisk of the Political Martyrs' Monument, which commemorates those who suffered in the fight for electoral reform in the 1790s. In the southern corner is the massive cylindrical stone tomb of David Hume (1711–76), Scotland's most famous philosopher. Hume was a noted atheist, prompting rumours that he had made a Faustian pact with the devil; after his death his friends held a vigil at the tomb for eight nights, burning candles and firing pistols into the darkness lest evil spirits should come to bear away his soul. (Waterloo Pl; ⊘8am-dusk; 🚍all Princes St buses)

Burns Monument MONUMENT

9 ⊙ Map p74, H4

The neoclassical Burns Monument (1830), a Greek-style memorial to Scotland's national poet Robert Burns, stands on the southern flank of Calton Hill. It was designed by Thomas Hamilton, a former pupil of the Royal High School (now closed), which stands just across the road. (Regent Rd)

Edinburgh Printmakers' Workshop & Gallery GALLERY

10 ⊙ Map p74, F2

Founded in 1967, this was the UK's first 'open-access' printmaking studio, providing studio space and equipment for professional artists and beginners alike. You can watch printmakers at work in the ground-floor studio, while the 1st-floor gallery hosts exhibitions of lithographs and screen prints by local artists. (📞557 2479; www.edinburgh -printmakers.co.uk; 23 Union St; admission free; ⊘10am-6pm Tue-Sat, closed 24 Dec– 9 Jan; 🚍8)

FRANCESCO DAMIN/GETTY IMAGES ©

Monuments on Calton Hill (p77)

Understand
Literary Edinburgh

Sir Walter Scott

The writer most deeply associated with Edinburgh is undoubtedly Sir Walter Scott (1771–1832), Scotland's greatest and most prolific novelist, best remembered for classic tales such as *The Antiquary, The Heart of Midlothian, Ivanhoe, Redgauntlet* and *Castle Dangerous*. The son of an Edinburgh lawyer, he lived at various New Town addresses before moving to his country house at Abbotsford.

Robert Louis Stevenson

Another Edinburgh novelist with an international reputation, Robert Louis Stevenson (1850–94) was born at 8 Howard Pl, in the New Town, into a family of famous lighthouse engineers. Stevenson is known and loved around the world for stories such as *Kidnapped, Catriona, Treasure Island, The Master of Ballantrae* and *The Strange Case of Dr Jekyll and Mr Hyde*, many of which have been made into successful films. The most popular and enduring is *Treasure Island* (1883), which has been translated into many different languages and has never been out of print.

Muriel Spark

No list of Edinburgh novelists would be complete without mention of Dame Muriel Spark (1918–2006), who was born in Edinburgh and educated at James Gillespie's High School for Girls, an experience that provided material for her best-known novel *The Prime of Miss Jean Brodie* (1961), a shrewd portrait of 1930s Edinburgh. Dame Muriel was a prolific writer; her 22nd novel, *The Finishing School*, was published in 2004 when she was 86.

Contemporary Writers

Walk into any bookshop in Edinburgh and you'll find a healthy 'Scottish Fiction' section, its shelves bulging with recently published works by best-selling Edinburgh authors such as Iain Banks, Christopher Brookmyre, Ian Rankin, Alexander McCall Smith and Irvine Welsh.

Ian Rankin's Rebus novels are dark, engrossing mysteries that explore the darker side of Scotland's capital city, filled with sharp dialogue, telling detail and three-dimensional characters.

Although she was born in Bristol, the publishing phenomenon that is JK Rowling famously began her career by penning the first Harry Potter adventure while nursing a coffee in various Edinburgh cafes; she still lives in the city.

Mansfield Place Church   CHURCH

11 ⊚ Map p74, E1

In complete contrast to the auster-ity of most of Edinburgh's religious buildings, this 19th-century, neo-Romanesque church contains a re-markable series of Renaissance-style frescoes painted in the 1890s by Irish-born artist Phoebe Anna Traquair (1852–1936). The murals have been restored and are on view to the public (check the website for any changes to viewing times). (www.mansfieldtraquair. org.uk; Mansfield Pl; admission free; ⊙1-4pm 2nd Sun of the month, 11am-1pm Sun-Thu during Edinburgh Festival Fringe; 🚌8)

Eating

Gardener's Cottage   SCOTTISH ££

12 🍽 Map p74, H2

This country cottage in the heart of the city, bedecked with flowers and fairy lights, offers one of Edinburgh's most interesting dining experiences – two tiny rooms with communal tables made of salvaged timber, and a set menu based on fresh local produce (most of the vegetables and fruit are grown in an organic garden in the city suburbs). Booking essential. (📞558 1221; www.thegardenerscottage.co; 1 Royal Terrace Gardens, London Rd; set menu lunch £15, dinner £25; ⊙lunch & dinner Thu-Mon, brunch Sat & Sun; 🚌all London Rd buses)

Locanda de Gusti   ITALIAN ££

13 🍽 Map p74, E1

This bustling bistro, loud with the buzz of conversation and the clink of glasses and cutlery, is no ordinary Ital-ian, but a little corner of cosmopolitan Naples complete with hearty Neapoli-tan home cooking by friendly head chef Rosario. The food ranges from light and tasty *pasta fresca* (ravioli tossed with butter and sage) to deli-cious platters of grilled langoustine, sea bream and sea bass. (📞558 9581; www.locandadegusti.com; 7-11 East London St; mains £12-19; ⊙lunch Mon, lunch & dinner Tue-Fri, noon-10.30pm Sat; 🍴; 🚌8)

The Dogs   BRITISH ££

14 🍽 Map p74, C3

One of the coolest tables in town, this bistro-style place uses cheaper cuts of meat and less-well-known, more-sustainable species of fish to create hearty, no-nonsense dishes such as lamb sweetbreads on toast, baked coley with *skirlie* (fried oatmeal and onion), and devilled liver with bacon and onions. (📞220 1208; www.thedogs online.co.uk; 110 Hanover St; mains £9-13; ⊙noon-4pm & 5-10pm; 🚌23, 27)

Café Marlayne   FRENCH ££

15 🍽 Map p74, C4

All weathered wood and candlelit tables, Café Marlayne is a cosy nook offering French farmhouse cooking – *brandade de morue* (salt cod) with green salad, slow-roast rack of lamb,

Diners at The Dogs (p81)

boudin noir (black pudding) with scallops and sautéed potato – at very reasonable prices. Booking recommended. (☎226 2230; www.cafemarlayne. com; 76 Thistle St; mains £12-15; ☺noon-10pm; 🚌24, 29, 42)

Broughton Deli
CAFE £

16 🍴 Map p74, E2

Mismatched cafe tables and chairs in a bright, attractive back room behind the deli counter provide an attractive setting for weekend brunch just off the main drag of the New Town's bohemian Broughton St. Brunch (served till 2pm, or 3pm on Sunday) includes American-style pancakes, veggie fry-ups, and poached eggs on toast with organic smoked salmon. (☎558 7111; www.broughton-deli.co.uk; 7 Barony St; mains £6-10; ☺8am-7.30pm Mon-Sat, 11am-5pm Sun; 🛜🖉; 🚌8)

Centotre
ITALIAN ££

A palatial Georgian banking hall enlivened with fuchsia-pink banners and aubergine booths is home to this lively, child-friendly Italian bar and restaurant (see **43** 🔒 Map p74, B4), where the emphasis is on fresh, authentic ingredients (produce imported weekly from Milan, homemade bread and pasta), and uncomplicated enjoyment of food. (☎225 1550; www.centotre.com; 103 George St; mains £13-20; ☺7.30am-midnight Mon-Sat, 10am-10pm Sun; 🛜🖉👶; 🚌all Princes St buses)

L'Escargot Bleu

FRENCH **££**

17 🍴 Map p74, E1

This cute little bistro is as Gallic as garlic but makes fine use of quality Scottish produce – the French-speaking staff will lead you knowledgeably through a menu that includes authentic Savoyard *tartiflette*, *quenelle* of pike with lobster sauce, and pigs' cheeks braised in red wine with roast winter vegetables. Two-course lunch and early-bird menu (5.30pm to 7pm) is £13. (☑556 1600; www.lescargotbleu.co.uk; 56 Broughton St; mains £13-18; ☺lunch & dinner Mon-Sat; 🚻8)

Urban Angel

CAFE **££**

18 🍴 Map p74, C3

A wholesome deli that puts the emphasis on fair-trade, organic and locally sourced produce, Urban Angel is also a delightfully informal cafe-bistro that serves all-day brunch (porridge with honey, French toast, eggs Benedict), tapas and a wide range of light, snacky meals. (☑225 6215; www.urban-angel.co.uk; 121 Hanover St; mains £5-13; ☺9am-5pm Mon-Sat, 10am-5pm Sun; 🍴🚻; 🚌23, 27)

Fishers in the City

SEAFOOD **££**

19 🍴 Map p74, C4

This more sophisticated version of the famous Fishers Bistro (p116) in Leith, with its granite-topped tables, warm yellow walls and a nautical theme, specialises in superior Scottish seafood – the knowledgeable staff serve up plump and succulent oysters, meltingly sweet scallops, and sea bass that's been grilled to perfection. (☑225 5109; www.fishersbistros.co.uk; 58 Thistle St; mains £14-20; ☺noon 10.30pm; 🛜🚻; 🚌13, 19, 37, 41)

21212

FRENCH **£££**

20 🍴 Map p74, H2

A grand Georgian town house on the side of Calton Hill is the elegant setting for this Michelin-starred restaurant – the name comes from the arrangement of menu choices. Divine decor by Timorous Beasties and Ralph Lauren provide the backdrop to an exquisitely prepared five-course dinner that is characterised by intriguing blends of multi-layered flavours and textures. (☑523 1030; www.21212restaurant.co.uk; 3 Royal Tce; 3 /5-course dinner £48/68; ☺lunch & dinner Tue-Sat; 🛜; 🚌all London Rd buses)

🔍 Local Life
Bohemian Broughton

The lively, bohemian district of Broughton, centred on Broughton St at the northeastern corner of the New Town, is the focus of Edinburgh's gay scene and home to many good bars, cafes and restaurants. The gay-friendly **Blue Moon Cafe** (Map p74, E2; ☑556 2788; 1 Barony St; mains £7-10; ☺11am-10pm Mon-Fri, 10am-10pm Sat & Sun) is a good place to find out what's happening in the neighbourhood.

Understand
The One O'Clock Gun

On Princes St you can tell locals and visitors apart by their reaction to the sudden explosion that rips through the air each day at one o'clock. Locals check their watches, while visitors shy like startled ponies. It's the One O'Clock Gun, fired from Mills Mount Battery on the castle battlements at 1pm sharp every day except Sunday.

The gun's origins date from the mid-19th century, when the accurate setting of a ship's chronometer was essential for safe navigation. The city authorities installed a time-signal on top of the Nelson Monument that was visible to ships anchored in the Firth of Forth. The gun was added as an audible signal that could be used when rain or mist obscured the ball. An interesting little exhibition in the Museum of Edinburgh (p40) details the gun's history and workings.

Drinking

Bramble   COCKTAIL BAR

21 🚇 Map p74, B3

One of those places that easily earns the sobriquet 'best-kept secret', Bramble is an unmarked cellar bar where a maze of stone and brick hideaways conceals what is arguably the city's best cocktail bar. No beer taps, no fuss, just expertly mixed drinks. (www.bramblebar.co.uk; 16a Queen St; 🚌 23, 27)

Café Royal Circle Bar   PUB

22 🚇 Map p74, E4

Perhaps *the* classic Edinburgh pub, the Café Royal's main claims to fame are its magnificent oval bar and the series of Doulton tile portraits of famous Victorian inventors. There are cosy semicircular booths, no fewer than seven Scottish ales on tap, and

there's excellent pub grub too. (www.caferoyaledinburgh.co.uk; 17 West Register St; 🚌 all Princes St buses)

Joseph Pearce's   PUB

23 🚇 Map p74, G1

A traditional Victorian pub that has been remodeled and given a new lease of life by Swedish owners, Pearce's has become a real hub of the local community, with good food (very family friendly before 5pm), a relaxed atmosphere, and events like Monday-night Scrabble games and summer crayfish parties. (📞 556 4140; www.bodabar.com; 23 Elm Row; 👶; 🚌 all Leith Walk buses)

Guildford Arms   PUB

24 🚇 Map p74, E4

Located next door to the Café Royal Circle Bar, the Guildford is another classic Victorian pub full of polished mahogany, gleaming brass and ornate cornices. The range of real ales is excellent – try to get a table in the unusual upstairs gallery, with a view over the sea of drinkers below. (www.guildfordarms.com; 1 West Register St; all Princes St buses)

Cumberland Bar PUB

25 Map p74, C1

Immortalised as the stereotypical New Town pub in Alexander McCall Smith's serialised novel *44 Scotland Street*, the Cumberland has an authentic, traditional wood-brass-and-mirrors look (despite being relatively new) and serves cask-conditioned ales and a wide range of malt whiskies. There's also a pleasant little beer garden outside. (www.cumberlandbar.co.uk; 1-3 Cumberland St; ; 23, 27)

Oxford Bar PUB

26 Map p74, A4

The Oxford is that rarest of things: a real pub for real people, with no 'theme', no music, no frills and no pretensions. 'The Ox' has been immortalised by Ian Rankin, author of the Inspector Rebus novels, whose fictional detective is a regular here; the author himself also makes the occasional visit. (www.oxfordbar.co.uk; 8 Young St; 19, 36, 37, 41, 47)

Amicus Apple COCKTAIL BAR

27 Map p74, C4

This laid-back cocktail lounge is the hippest hang-out in the New Town,

popular with well-heeled students. The drinks menu ranges from retro classics such as Bloody Marys and mojitos, to original and unusual concoctions such as the Cuillin Martini (Tanqueray No 10 gin, Talisker malt whisky and smoked rosemary). (15 Frederick St; ; all Princes St buses)

Kay's Bar PUB

28 Map p74, A3

Housed in a former wine merchant's office, tiny Kay's Bar is a cosy haven with plush red banquettes, a coal fire and a fine range of real ales. Good food is served in the back room at lunchtime, but you'll have to book a

Local Life
Edinburgh Zoo

Opened in 1913, **Edinburgh Zoo** (www.edinburghzoo.org.uk; 134 Corstorphine Rd; adult/child £16/11.50; 9am-6pm Apr-Sep, to 5pm Oct & Mar, to 4.30pm Nov-Feb; 12, 26, 31) is one of the world's leading conservation zoos. Edinburgh's captive breeding program has helped save many endangered species, including Siberian tigers, pygmy hippos and red pandas. The main attractions are the penguin parade (the zoo's penguins go for a walk every day at 2.15pm), the sea lion training session (daily at 11.15am), and the two giant pandas, Tian Tian and Yang Guang, which arrived in December 2011.

Top Tip

Edinburgh Trams

Edinburgh's new tram line, scheduled to begin operation in summer 2014, runs from the airport to York Pl (at the top of Leith Walk), via Murrayfield, Haymarket and Princes St. More information is available at www.edinburgh trams.com.

table – Kay's is a popular spot. (www. kaysbar.co.uk; 39 Jamaica St; 🚌24, 29, 42)

Elbow   BAR

29 Map p74, E1

An attractive mix of modern and retro style makes Elbow one of the New Town's most appealing neighbourhood bars, with staff who make you feel welcome, a tempting menu of wines and cocktails, and regular pub quizzes and live music nights. (☑556 5662; www.elbowedinburgh.co.uk; 133-135 E Claremont St; 🛜 👶; 🚌36)

Tigerlily   COCKTAIL BAR

30 Map p74, A4

Swirling textured wallpapers, glittering chainmail curtains, crystal chandeliers and plush pink and gold sofas have won a cluster of design awards for this boutique hotel bar, where sharp suits and stiletto heels line the banquettes. There's expertly mixed cocktails, as well as Japanese Kirin beer on draught and Innis & Gunn Scottish ale in bottles. (☑225 5005;

www.tigerlilyedinburgh.co.uk; 125 George St; 🛜; 🚌all Princes St buses)

Entertainment

Jam House   LIVE MUSIC

31 ⭐ Map p74, D3

The brainchild of rhythm'n'blues pianist and TV personality Jools Holland, the Jam House is set in a former BBC TV studio and offers a combination of fine dining and live jazz and blues performances. Admission is for over-21s only, and there's a smart-casual dress code. (☑226 4380; www. thejamhouse.com; 5 Queen St; admission £6, free before 8pm; ⏰6pm-3am Fri & Sat; 🚌all York Pl buses)

The Stand Comedy Club   COMEDY

32 ⭐ Map p74, E3

The Stand, founded in 1995, is Edinburgh's main independent comedy venue. It's an intimate cabaret bar with performances every night and a free Sunday lunchtime show. (☑558 7272; www.thestand.co.uk; 5 York Pl; admission £2-10; 🚌all York Pl buses)

Lulu   CLUB

Lush leather sofas, red satin cushions, fetishistic steel-mesh curtains and dim red lighting all help to create a decadent atmosphere in this drop-dead-gorgeous club venue beneath the Tigerlily boutique hotel (see 30 Map p74, A4). Resident and guest DJs show a bit more originality than at your average club. (www.luluedinburgh. co.uk; 125 George St; ☒19, 36, 37, 41, 47)

Opal Lounge CLUB

33 ⭐ Map p74, C4

The Opal Lounge is jammed at weekends with affluent 20-somethings who've spent £200 and two hours in front of a mirror to achieve that artlessly scruffy look. During the week, when the air-kissing crowds thin out, it's a good place to relax with an expensive but expertly mixed cocktail. Expect to queue on weekend evenings. (www.opallounge.co.uk; 51 George St; ☒19, 36, 37, 41, 47)

Voodoo Rooms LIVE MUSIC

34 ⭐ Map p74, E4

Decadent decor of black leather, ornate plasterwork and gilt detailing create a funky setting for this complex of bars and performance spaces above the Café Royal that host everything from classic soul and Motown to Vegas lounge-club nights (www.vegasscotland.co.uk) to live local bands. (☎556 7060; www.thevoodoorooms. com; 19a West Register St; admission free-£10; ☺noon-1am Fri-Sun, 4pm-1am Mon-Thu; ☒all Princes St buses)

CC Blooms CLUB

35 ⭐ Map p74, G2

New owners have given the long-established queen of Edinburgh's gay scene a shot in the arm – it's now a sophisticated cafe-bar by day, and a

classy club with two floors of deafening dance and disco by night. (☎556 9331; ccbloomsedinburgh.com; 23 Greenside Pl; admission free; ☺11am-3am Mon-Sat, 12.30pm-3am Sun; ☒all Leith Walk buses)

Edinburgh Playhouse MUSIC

36 ⭐ Map p74, G2

This restored theatre at the top of Leith Walk stages Broadway musicals, dance shows, opera and concerts. (www. edinburgh-playhouse.co.uk; 18-22 Greenside Pl; ☺box office 10am-6pm Mon-Sat, to 8pm show nights; ☒all Leith Walk buses)

Shopping

One World Shop HANDICRAFTS

37 🅐 Map p74, A5

Stocks a wide range of handmade crafts from developing countries, including paper goods, rugs, textiles, jewellery, ceramics, accessories and food and drink, all from accredited fair-trade suppliers. During the festival period (when the shop stays open

---

☑ Top Tip

Late Shopping Days

Most shops in Edinburgh open late on Thursdays, till 7pm or 8pm. Many city-centre stores extend their late opening to all weekdays during the Edinburgh Festival in August and during the three weeks before Christmas.

till 6pm) there's a crafts fair in the churchyard outside. (www.oneworldshop. co.uk; St John's Church, Princes St; 🚍 all Princes St buses)

Lime Blue
JEWELLERY

38 🔒 Map p74, B4

Put on your shades and tighten your grip on that purse – you'll be dazzled by both the merchandise and the pricetags in this elegant and clean-cut jewellery emporium, with diamond-encrusted necklaces and rings by Leo Pizzo, finely crafted brooches by Picchiotti and watches by Versace. Downstairs you'll find a broad range of silver jewellery, crystalware and other luxury goods. (📞220 2164; www. lime-blue.co.uk; 107 George St; 🕙10am-6pm Mon-Wed & Fri, to 7pm Thu, noon-5pm Sun; 🚍19, 36, 37, 41, 47)

Scottish Gallery
ARTS & CRAFTS

39 🔒 Map p74, C2

Home to Edinburgh's leading art dealers, Aitken Dott, this private gallery exhibits and sells paintings by contemporary Scottish artists and the masters of the late 19th and early 20th centuries (including the Scottish

---

✅ Top Tip

Shopping Guide

The official Edinburgh Shopper website (www.edinburghshopper. com) is a useful guide to Edinburgh's main retail areas and newly opened shops.

Colourists), as well as a wide range of ceramics, glassware, jewellery and textiles. (📞558 1200; www.scottish-gallery. co.uk; 16 Dundas St; 🕙10am-6pm Mon-Fri, to 4pm Sat; 🚍23, 27)

McNaughtan's Bookshop
BOOKS

40 🔒 Map p74, G1

The maze of shelves at McNaughtan's Bookshop (established in 1957) houses a broad spectrum of general secondhand and antiquarian books, with good selections of Scottish, history, travel, art and architecture, and children's books. (📞556 5897; www. mcnaughtansbookshop.com; 3a-4a Haddington Pl; 🕙11am-5pm Tue-Sat; 🚍all Leith Walk buses)

Valvona & Crolla
FOOD & DRINK

41 🔒 Map p74, G1

The acknowledged queen of Edinburgh delicatessens, established during the 1930s, Valvona & Crolla is packed with Mediterranean goodies, including an excellent choice of fine wines. It also has a good cafe. (📞556 6066; www.valvonacrolla.co.uk; 19 Elm Row; 🕙8.30am-6pm Mon-Thu, 8am-6.30pm Fri & Sat, 10.30am-4pm Sun; 🚍all Leith Walk buses)

Oscar & Fitch
FASHION

42 🔒 Map p74, E3

If you're looking for some stylish spectacles, this boutique stocks the city's largest selection of designer eyewear, from head-turningly avant-garde daytime glasses to popstar-cool shades,

VISITBRITAIN/NATALIE PECHT ©

Valvona & Crolla

all expertly fitted to your personal satisfaction. ($556 6461; www.oscarand fitch.com; 20 Multrees Walk; ⏰10am-6pm Mon-Wed, Fri & Sat, to 7pm Thu, 11am-5pm Sun; 🚌all St Andrew Sq buses)

Whistles
FASHION

43 🔒 Map p74, B4

Crisp white and hot pink decor sets off the racks of designer clothes for women in this branch of the well-known London-based store. Lots of little black dresses here – just the place if you're looking for something a little more formal for that special occasion – as well as quirky and offbeat styles. ($226 4398; www.whistles.co.uk; 97 George St; ⏰10am-6pm Mon-Wed, Fri & Sat, to 7pm Thu, noon-5pm Sun; 🚌19, 36, 37, 41, 47)

Fopp
MUSIC

44 🔒 Map p74, D4

Despite the financial ups and downs of parent company HMV, the classic Fopp record store continues as one of Edinburgh's best places to hunt for cheap CDs and vinyl, and the friendly staff really know what they're talking about. ($220 0310; 7 Rose St; ⏰9.30am-7pm Mon-Sat, 11am-6pm Sun; 🚌all Princes St buses)

Jo Malone
BEAUTY

45 🔒 Map p74, B4

This sweet smelling palace of posh cosmetics has instore experts offering a 'fragrance combining' consultation that will allow you to choose your perfect perfume, along with a range of other scents to 'layer' over it. Try the original nutmeg and ginger bath oil that made Ms Malone famous, or other intriguing combinations such as lime, basil and mandarin, or amber and lavender. ($478 8555; www.jomalone. co.uk; 93 George St; ⏰10am-6pm Mon-Wed, to 7pm Thu, 9.30am-6pm Fri & Sat, noon-5pm Sun; 🚌19, 36, 37, 41)

Palenque
JEWELLERY

46 🔒 Map p74, B4

Palenque is a treasure trove of contemporary silver jewellery and handcrafted accessories made using ceramics, textiles and metalwork. (www.palenquejewellery.co.uk; 99 Rose St; 🚌all Princes St buses)

Explore

West End & Dean Village

Edinburgh's West End is an extension of the New Town, with elegant Georgian terraces, garden squares and an enclave of upmarket shops along William St and Stafford St. It takes in the Exchange district, now the city's financial powerhouse, and the theatre quarter on Lothian Rd, and in the west tumbles downhill into the valley of the Water of Leith to meet the picturesque Dean Village.

The Sights in a Day

☀ Enjoy breakfast with the newspapers at **Indigo Yard** (p97), then take a stroll among the fashion boutiques of Stafford St and William St before heading down to **Dean Village** (p95; pictured left). Follow the Water of Leith Walkway upstream to the **Scottish National Gallery of Modern Art** (p92), and plan on having lunch at **Cafe Modern One** (p93).

☀ Spend the afternoon admiring the modern masterpieces at the gallery's two major exhibition spaces – don't forget to allow time to explore the outdoor sculptures and landscape art in the gallery grounds. Then head back uphill to the West End via Belford Rd and Palmerston Pl for a relaxing pint of real ale at **Bert's Bar** (p97)

☾ Book a pre-theatre dinner – at **Kanpai** (p95) for sushi, or **Escargot Blanc** (p96) for French cuisine – and then take in a performance at the **Traverse** (p99) or **Lyceum** (p99) theatre. Or, if you'd prefer some traditional Scottish entertainment, go for dinner and a *ceilidh* (evening of traditional Scottish music and dancing) at the **Ghillie Dhu** (p97).

👁 Top Sights

Scottish National Gallery of Modern Art (p92)

♥ Best of Edinburgh

Eating
Castle Terrace (p95)
McKirdy's Steakhouse (p97)

Shopping
Edinburgh Farmers Market (p96)

Museums & Galleries
Scottish National Gallery of Modern Art (p92)

Getting There

🚌 **Bus** Lothian Buses 3, 4, 12, 25, 26, 31, 33 and 44 head west from Princes St to the West End, going along Shandwick Pl to Haymarket. For Dean Village, take bus 19, 36, 37, 41 or 47 from George St to Dean Bridge and walk down Bell's Brae.

Top Sights
Scottish National Gallery of Modern Art

Edinburgh's gallery of modern art is split between two impressive neoclassical buildings surrounded by landscaped grounds some 500m west of Dean Village. As well as showcasing a stunning collection of paintings by the popular, post-Impressionist Scottish Colourists – in *Reflections, Balloch,* Leslie Hunter pulls off the improbable trick of making Scotland look like the south of France – the gallery is the starting point for a walk along the Water of Leith, following a trail of sculptures by Antony Gormley.

Map p94, A2

www.nationalgalleries.org

75 Belford Rd

fee for special exhibitions

10am-5pm

13

Don't Miss

Modern One

The main collection, known as Modern One, concentrates on 20th-century art, with various European movements represented by the likes of Matisse, Picasso, Kirchner, Magritte, Miró, Mondrian and Giacometti. American and English artists are also represented, but most space is given to Scottish painters – from the Scottish Colourists of the early 20th century to contemporary artists such as Peter Howson and Ken Currie.

Modern Two

Directly across Belford Rd from Modern One, another neoclassical mansion (formerly an orphanage) houses its annexe, Modern Two, which is home to a large collection of sculpture and graphic art created by the Edinburgh-born artist Sir Eduardo Paolozzi. One of the 1st-floor rooms houses a re-creation of Paolozzi's studio, while the rest of the building stages temporary exhibitions.

The Grounds

The gallery's collection extends to the surrounding grounds, featuring sculptures by Henry Moore, Rachel Whiteread, Julian Opie and Barbara Hepworth, among others, as well as a sensuous 'landform artwork' by Charles Jencks.

Water of Leith

A path and stairs at the rear of the gallery lead to the Water of Leith Walkway, which you can follow downstream for 4 miles to Leith. This takes you past **6 Times**, a sculptural project by Antony Gormley comprising five human figures standing at points along the river (the sixth sprouts from the pavement at the gallery entrance). The river statues are designed to fall over in flood conditions, so some of them may not be visible after heavy rain.

☑ Top Tips

▶ A free shuttle bus runs between here and the Scottish National Gallery on the Mound, with hourly departures from 11am to 5pm.

▶ The Scottish National Galleries' ArtHunter smartphone app allows you to 'capture' and examine high-res images of artworks (there are monthly themes), which then give access to video and audio content about the artists and their creations.

✗ Take a Break

Each part of the gallery has its own eatery: **Cafe Modern One** (mains £6-8; ⊙9am-4.30pm Mon-Fri, 10am-4.30pm Sat & Sun; 🛜👪) has an outdoor terrace overlooking the sculptures in the grounds, while **Cafe Modern Two** (mains £6-8; ⊙10am-4.30pm Mon-Sat, 11am-4.30pm Sun; 🛜) is a based on a belle epoque Viennese coffee house. Both serve cakes and coffee, plus hot lunch dishes from noon till 2.30pm.

400 m

0.2 miles

E

Heriot Row

Queen Street Gardens

Queen St

Hill St

Castle St

Rose St

Princes St

Young St

Charlotte Sq

Castle St

West Princes Street Gardens

King's Stables Rd

Castle Tce

Spittal St

Grindlay St

3

17 20

16

4

15

Lothian Rd

D

Moray Pl

Charlotte Square

W Approach Rd

Morrison St

Canning St

11

8 14 13

5

Queensferry St

Shandwick Pl

12 18

19

9

6

Torphichen St

7

WEST END

Manor Pl

William St

W Maitland St

Morrison St

Chester St

Walker St

C

Eton Tce

Water of Leith

Dean Bridge

1

Dean Gardens

2

Dean Village

Rothesay Pl

Palmerston Pl

10

B

Queensferry Rd

Buckingham Tce

Belgrave Cres

Dean Path

Belford Rd

Douglas Cres

Glencairn Cres

Haymarket Tce

Haymarket Station

Dalry Rd

A

Dean Cemetery

Ravelston Tce

Scottish National Gallery of Modern Art

Belford Pl

Ravelston Park

1

2

3

4

For reviews see	
◆ Top Sights	p92
◎ Sights	p95
◎ Eating	p95
◎ Drinking	p97
◎ Entertainment	p98
◎ Shopping	p99

Sights

Dean Bridge
BRIDGE

1 Map p94, C1

Designed by Thomas Telford and built between 1829 and 1832 to allow the New Town to expand to the northwest, the Dean Bridge vaults gracefully over the narrow, steep-sided valley of the Water of Leith. (🚌19, 36, 37, 41, 47)

Dean Village
NEIGHBOURHOOD

2 💿 Map p94, C2

Down in the valley, just west of the Dean Bridge, is Dean Village (dene is a Scots word for valley). The village was founded as a milling community by the canons of Holyrood Abbey in the 12th century and by 1700 there were 11 water mills here, grinding grain for flour. One of the old mill buildings has been converted into flats, and the village is now an attractive residential area. (🚌19, 36, 37, 41, 47)

Eating

Castle Terrace
SCOTTISH £££

3 ✗ Map p94, E3

Little more than a year after opening in 2010, TV chef Tom Kitchin's second Edinburgh restaurant, under chef-patron Dominic Jack, was awarded a Michelin star. The menu is seasonal and applies sharply whetted Parisian skills to the finest of local produce, be it Ayrshire pork, Aberdeenshire lamb or Newhaven crab – even the cheese in the sauces is Scottish. (📞229 1222; www.castleterracerestaurant.com; 33-35 Castle Tce; mains £25-34, 3-course lunch £26.50; ⏰lunch & dinner Tue Sat; 🚇2)

Kanpai
JAPANESE ££

4 ✗ Map p94, E4

The latest sushi restaurant to open in Edinburgh goes straight to the top of the charts with its minimalist interior, fresh, top-quality fish and elegantly presented dishes – the squid tempura comes in a delicate woven basket, while the sashimi combo is presented as a flower arrangement in an ice-filled stoneware bowl. (📞228 1602;

LONELY PLANET/GETTY IMAGES ©

Dean Bridge

Local Life
Edinburgh Farmers Market

Every Saturday, against the impressive backdrop of the castle crags, the city's **farmers market** (Map p94, E3; 📞 652 5940; www.edinburghfarmersmarket.com; Castle Tce; ⏱9am-2pm Sat; 🚌all Lothian Rd buses) is lined with stalls selling everything from heather honey to handmade cheeses, home-reared venison, smoked trout, seasonal wild game, and organic eggs from rare-breed hens.

www.kanpaisushi.co.uk; 8-10 Grindlay St; mains £8-14, sushi per piece £4-7; ⏱lunch & dinner Tue-Sun; 🚌all Lothian Rd buses)

Escargot Blanc   FRENCH ££

5 🍴 Map p94, D2

This superb neighbourhood bistro, with French chef and waitstaff, and two-thirds of its top-quality produce sourced in Scotland (one-third is imported from France), is a true 'Auld Alliance' of culinary cultures. Choose from a menu of classics such as escargots in garlic, parsley and hazelnut butter, *coq au vin* (made with free-range Scottish chicken) and perfectly prepared Scottish ribeye steak with *bleu d'Auvergne* sauce. (📞226 1890; www.lescargotblanc.co.uk; 17 Queensferry St; ⏱noon-3pm & 5.30-10pm Mon-Thu, noon-3pm & 5.30- 10.30pm Fri & Sat; 🚌19, 36, 37, 41, 47)

Cafe Milk   CAFE £

6 🍴 Map p94, C4

This is fast food with a conscience – natural, nutritious, locally sourced and freshly prepared, from organic porridge to courgette, lemon and feta fritters, to North Indian dhal with rice or flatbread. Take away, or sit in and soak up a retro vibe with old Formica tables, battered school benches, enamel plates and junkshop cutlery stacked in golden-syrup tins. (www.cafemilk.co.uk; 232 Morrison St; mains £3-6; ⏱7.30am-4pm Mon-Fri, 8am-4pm Sat, 8am-3pm Sun; 📶🖊; 🚌2, 3, 4, 25, 33 or 44)

Chop Chop   CHINESE £

7 🍴 Map p94, C4

Chop Chop is a Chinese restaurant with a difference, in that it serves dishes popular in China rather than Britain – as its slogan says, 'Can a billion people be wrong?' No sweet-and-sour pork here, but a range of delicious dumplings filled with pork and coriander, beef and chilli or lamb and leek, and unusual vegetarian dishes such as aubergine fried with garlic and Chinese spices. (📞221 1155; www.chop-chop.co.uk; 248 Morrison St; mains £8-11; ⏱lunch & dinner; 🖊; 🚌2, 3, 4, 25, 33, 44)

La P'tite Folie   FRENCH ££

8 🍴 Map p94, D2

Housed in an unusual, Tudor-lookalike building, La P'tite Folie is a cosy French restaurant tucked in an upstairs dining room with green walls, dark wood and a pleasantly clubbish atmosphere – try to grab the table in the little corner turret with its view of the spires of St Mary's Cathedral. Two-course lunch £10.50. (☎225 8678; www.laptitefolie.co.uk; 9 Randolph Pl; mains £13-26; ⏰noon-3pm & 6-11pm Mon-Sat; 🚌19, 36, 37, 41, 47)

McKirdy's Steakhouse

SCOTTISH ££

9 Map p94, D4

The McKirdy brothers – owners of a local butcher's business established in 1895 – have cut out the middleman and now run one of Edinburgh's best steakhouses. The friendly staff here serve up starters – such as haggis with Drambuie sauce – and juicy, perfectly cooked steaks from rump to T-bone, accompanied by mustard mash or crispy fries. (☎229 6660; www.mckirdyssteakhouse.co.uk; 151 Morrison St; mains £11-26; ⏰5.30-10pm Sun-Thu, 5-10.30pm Fri & Sat; 👪; 🚌2)

Omar Khayyam

INDIAN ££

10 Map p94, C4

This is a modern Punjabi restaurant with attentive, waistcoated waiters, stylish modern decor and an unusual water feature trickling away in the middle of the dining room. The food is always fresh and flavourful, ranging from old favourites such as chicken tikka masala to more unusual dishes like Kabul chicken (with chickpeas, cumin and coriander). (☎220 0024; www.omar-khayyam.co.uk; 1 Grosvenor St; mains £8-14; ⏰noon-2pm & 5pm-midnight Mon-Fri, noon-midnight Sat, 4.30pm-midnight Sun; 🥕👪; 🚌all Haymarket buses)

Drinking

Ghillie Dhu

PUB

11 Map p94, D3

This spectacular bar, with its huge, chunky, beer-hall tables, leather sofa booths and polished black-and-white tile floor, makes a grand setting for the live folk-music sessions that take place here most nights (admission free), plus a full Scottish *ceilidh* (evening of traditional music and dancing) every Friday at 7.30pm (£25 a head, including three-course dinner). (☎222 9930, www.ghillie dhu.co.uk; 2 Rutland Pl; ⏰noon-3am; 🚌all Princes St buses)

Bert's Bar

PUB

12 Map p94, C3

A classic re-creation of a 1930s-style pub – a welcoming womb with warm wood and leather decor, complete with a jar of pickled eggs on the bar. Bert's is a good place to sample real ale and down-to-earth pub grub such as Scotch pies with mashed potatoes, gravy and mushy peas. (☎225 5748; 29-31 William St; 📶; 🚌all Shandwick Pl buses)

Indigo Yard

BAR

13 Map p94, D2

Set around an airy, stone-floored and glass-roofed courtyard, Indigo Yard is a fashionable West End watering hole that has been patronised by the likes of Liam Gallagher, Pierce Brosnan and Kylie Minogue. Good food – including open-air barbecues during the summer months – just adds to the attraction. (☏ 220 5603; www.indigoyard edinburgh.co.uk; 7 Charlotte Lane; ☺ 8.30am-1am; 🛜 👪; 🚌 19, 36, 37, 41, 47)

Sygn
COCKTAIL BAR

14 🍸 Map p94, D2

The plush banquettes and sleek, polished tables in this sharply styled bar are just the place to pose with a passionfruit bellini or a glass of Pol Roger. The languid and laid-back atmosphere at this bar is complemented by cool tunes and superb cocktails, and the food menu is surprisingly good. (☏ 225 6060; www.sygn.co.uk; 15 Charlotte Lane; ☺ 10am-1am; 🛜; 🚌 19, 36, 37, 41, 47)

Entertainment

Filmhouse
CINEMA

15 ⭐ Map p94, E4

The Filmhouse is the main venue for the annual Edinburgh International Film Festival and screens a full program of art-house, classic, foreign and second-run films, with lots of themes, retrospectives and 70mm screenings. It has wheelchair access to all three

STEVE MORGAN/ALAMY ©

Edinburgh Farmers Market (p96)

screens. (www.filmhousecinema.com; 88 Lothian Rd; 📞; 🚌all Lothian Rd buses)

Traverse Theatre THEATRE, DANCE

16 ⭐ Map p94, E3

The Traverse is the main focus for new Scottish writing and stages an adventurous program of contemporary drama and dance. The box office only opens on Sunday (from 4pm) when there's a show on. (www.traverse.co.uk; 10 Cambridge St; ⏰box office 10am-6pm Mon-Sat, to 8pm show nights)

Royal Lyceum Theatre THEATRE, MUSIC

17 ⭐ Map p94, C4

This grand Victorian theatre stages drama, concerts, musicals and ballet. (www.lyceum.org.uk; 30b Grindlay St; ⏰box office 10am-6pm Mon-Sat, to 8pm show nights; ♿)

Shopping

Arkangel & Felon FASHION

18 🔒 Map p94, D3

Helpful staff will help you pick out a glamorous outfit from their carefully selected wardrobe of offbeat European chic and vintage fashion – look out for designer wear by Sarah Pacini and Ilse

Jacobsen, and jewellery by Mirabelle and Ritzy Crystal. (📞226 4466; www.arkangelandfelon.com; 4 William St; ⏰10am-5.30pm Mon-Wed, Fri & Sat, to 6.30pm Thu; 🚌all Shandwick Pl buses)

Helen Bateman SHOES

19 🔒 Map p94, D3

From sparkly stilettos and sleek satin pumps to 1950s-style open-sided court shoes and soft suede loafers, Helen Bateman's shop has every kind of handmade shoe and boot you could wish for. You can even order customised satin shoes – slingbacks, pumps or kitten heels – dyed to any colour and decorated with whatever your heart desires. (📞220 4495; www.helen bateman.com; 16 William St; ⏰9.30am-6pm Mon-Sat; 🚌all Shandwick Pl buses)

McAlister Matheson Music MUSIC

20 🔒 Map p94, E4

This is Scotland's biggest and most knowledgeable shop for classical music CDs, DVDs and books – just about every staff member seems to have a music degree. It also stocks a selection of Scottish folk and Celtic music. (📞228 3827; www.mmmusic.co.uk; 1 Grindlay St; ⏰9.30am-6pm Mon-Thu, 9.30am-6.30pm Fri, 9am-5.30pm Sat; 🚌2, 35)

Explore

Stockbridge

Stockbridge is a bohemian enclave to the north of the city centre, with an interesting selection of shops and a good choice of pubs and neighbourhood bistros. Originally a mill village, it was developed in the early 19th century on lands owned largely by the painter Sir Henry Raeburn, who gave his name to its main street, Raeburn Pl.

The Sights in a Day

☀ The best way to arrive in Stockbridge is by walking along the **Water of Leith**, starting from either Dean Village (10 minutes) or the Scottish National Gallery of Modern Art (25 minutes). Stroll the streets and browse the shops before enjoying lunch at one of the bistros in St Stephen St.

☀ Walk along the cobbled lane of St Bernard's Row, then Arboretum Ave and Arboretum Place to the **Royal Botanic Garden** (p102), and plan to spend the rest of the afternoon exploring its many attractions. Don't forget to grab a coffee at the **Terrace Cafe** (p103) and soak up the view of the castle.

☾ Stockbridge nightlife is decidedly low-key, consisting of tempting restaurants and laid-back bars. Grab a sofa in the **Stockbridge Tap** (p108) to enjoy the best of Scottish real ales.

For a local's day in Stockbridge, see p104.

👁 Top Sights
Royal Botanic Garden (p102)

🔍 Local Life
A Sunday Stroll Around Stockbridge (p104)

💗 Best of Edinburgh

Shopping
Galerie Mirages (p109)
Annie Smith (p108)
Stockbridge Market (p105)

Drinking
Stockbridge Tap (p108)

Getting There

🚌 **Bus** Lothian Buses 24, 29 and 42 run from Frederick St in the city centre to Raeburn Pl in Stockbridge. Buses 23 and 27 head down Dundas St to Brandon Tce for the Circle Cafe.

Top Sights
Royal Botanic Garden

Edinburgh's Royal Botanic Garden is the second-oldest institution of its kind in Britain (after Oxford's), and one of the most respected in the world. Founded near Holyrood in 1670 and moved to its present location in 1823, it has 70 beautifully landscaped acres that include splendid Victorian glasshouses, colourful swathes of rhododendron and azalea, and a world-famous rock garden.

👁 Map p106, D1

www.rbge.org.uk

Arboretum Pl

admission free

🕐10am-6pm Mar-Sep, to 5pm Feb & Oct, to 4pm Nov-Jan

🚌 8, 17, 23, 27

Victorian Palm House

Don't Miss

John Hope Gateway

The garden's new **visitor centre** is housed in this striking, environmentally friendly building overlooking the main Arboretum Pl entrance. There are exhibitions on biodiversity, climate change and sustainable development, as well as displays of rare plants from the institution's collection and a specially created biodiversity garden.

Glasshouses

A cluster of around 25 **glasshouses** (Inverleith Row; adult/child £4.50/1; ☻10am-5.30pm Mar-Sep, to 4.30pm Feb & Oct, to 3.30pm Nov-Jan) in the garden's northern corner houses a huge collection of tropical plants. Pride of place goes to the ornate **Victorian Palm House**, built in 1834 and home to vast rainforest palms, including a Bermudan palmetto that dates from 1822. The **Front Range** of 1960s designer glasshouses is famous for its tropical pond filled with giant Amazonian water lilies.

Rock Garden

Since it was first created in 1871, the rock garden has been one of the RBGE's most popular features. Boulders and scree slopes made from Scottish sandstone and conglomerate are home to more than 4000 species of alpine and subarctic plants from all over the world.

Sculptures

Pick up a map from the visitor centre so that you can track down the garden's numerous sculptures, ranging from a statue of Swedish botanist and taxonomist Carl Linnaeus (1707–78) by Scottish architect Robert Adam, to modern works by Yorkshire sculptor Barbara Hepworth and landscape artist Andy Goldsworthy.

☑ Top Tips

▶ Guided tours of the gardens (per person £5) depart at 11am and 2pm daily from April to October.

▶ The main entrance is the West Gate, on Arboretum Pl; however, city buses stop near the smaller East Gate on Inverleith Row. The Majestic Tour bus drops off and picks up at the West Gate.

▶ It's worth visiting the website before your visit to check out what the current month's seasonal highlights are.

✗ Take a Break

The **Gateway Restaurant** (www.gateway restaurant.net; mains £7-11; ☻9.30am-6pm Mon-Fri, 9am-6pm Sun) in the John Hope Gateway visitor centre serves hot breakfast and lunch dishes, while the **Terrace Cafe** (mains £5-8; ☻10am-5.30pm), in the middle of the gardens, has outdoor tables with a superb view of the city skyline.

Local Life
A Sunday Stroll Around Stockbridge

Just a short walk downhill from the city centre, Stockbridge feels a world away with its peaceful backstreets, leafy Georgian gardens, quirky boutiques and art galleries, with the Water of Leith flowing through the middle. There's a strong community spirit that really comes alive on Sundays, when Stockbridge Market attracts crowds of local shoppers and browsers.

❶ Breakfast at Circle

Any bus marked Canonmills will take you north along Hanover and Dundas streets to the **Circle Cafe** (www.thecirclecafe.com; 1 Brandon Tce; mains £5-10; ⏰8.30am-4.30pm Mon-Thu, to 10pm Fri & Sat, 9am-4.30pm Sun), a popular neighbourhood eatery famed for its lavish breakfasts. Choose from gourmet pastries, eggs Benedict, homemade potato scones or a full fry-up.

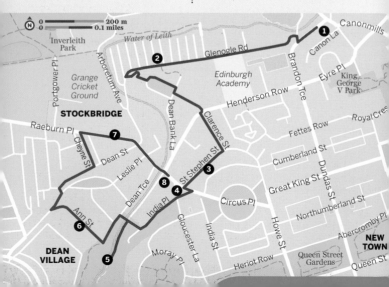

❷ Stockbridge Colonies

A short walk along Glenogle Rd leads to the Stockbridge Colonies, a series of terraced stone houses built by a workers' co-operative in the 19th century to provide affordable working class accommodation (now highly desirable and not so affordable).

❸ Browse St Stephen Street

St Stephen Street (www.ststephen street.com) is pure Stockbridge, a side street crammed with tiny galleries, boutiques, restaurants and basement bars. **RM Art** (www.rosiemckenzieart.com; 51 St Stephen St; ☺noon-6pm Wed-Fri, 11am-6pm Sat, 1-5pm Sun) specialises in works by up-and-coming local artists, while **Cherubim** (www.edinburgh-cherubim.co.uk; ☺11am-6pm Wed-Sat, to 5pm Sun) offers antique and secondhand furnishings. At St Stephen Pl, you can see the Georgian archway that once led to the old Stockbridge meat market.

❹ Gloucester Lane

This steep, cobbled street was once the main thoroughfare connecting Stockbridge to the city, before the New Town was built. **Duncan's Land**, at the corner with India Pl (now Songkran restaurant), is one of Stockbridge's oldest surviving buildings, dating from 1790, though it used masonry from demolished Old Town buildings (the lintel is dated 1605).

❺ St Bernard's Well

A short walk along the Water of Leith Walkway leads to **St Bernard's Well** (☺noon-3pm Sun, Aug only), a circular temple with a statue of Hygeia, the goddess of health, built in 1789. The sulphurous spring was discovered by schoolboys from George Heriot's School in 1760, and became hugely popular during the late-18th-century fad for 'taking the waters' – one visitor compared the taste to 'the washings of foul gun barrels'.

❻ Ann Street

The Georgian garden villas along Ann St (named after Sir Henry Raeburn's wife) are among the most beautiful and desirable houses in Edinburgh. The street is reckoned to be the most expensive in the city, and was named in 2008 as one of the UK's six most exclusive streets. It is also the setting for JM Barrie's 1902 novel *Quality Street*.

❼ Raeburn Place

Stockbridge's main drag is a bustle of shops, pubs and restaurants, with everything from chain stores and charity shops to craft shops, galleries and jewellery boutiques.

❽ Stockbridge Market

On Sundays, **Stockbridge Market** (www. stockbridgemarket.com; cnr Kerr St & Saunders St; ☺10am-5pm Sun) is the focus of the community, set in a leafy square next to the bridge that gives the district its name. Stalls range from fresh Scottish produce to handmade ceramics, jewellery, soaps and cosmetics. Grab an espresso from Steampunk Coffee, which operates out of a 1970s VW campervan.

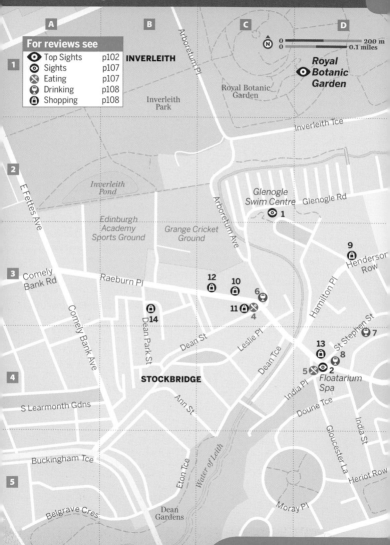

| A | B | C | D |

For reviews see
- 👁 Top Sights   p102
- ⊙ Sights   p107
- ✕ Eating   p107
- 🍷 Drinking   p108
- 🔒 Shopping   p108

INVERLEITH

Royal Botanic Garden

Royal Botanic Garden

Inverleith Park

Inverleith Tce

Arboretum Pl

200 m
0.1 miles

Inverleith Pond

Glenogle Swim Centre

Glenogle Rd

⊙ 1

Edinburgh Academy Sports Ground

Grange Cricket Ground

Arboretum Ave

9 🔒
Henderson Row

E Fettes Ave

Comely Bank Rd

Raeburn Pl

12 🔒

10 🔒

6
11 🔒 ✕
4

Hamilton Pl

St Stephen St

7

Comely Bank Ave

14 🔒

Dean Park St

Dean St

Leslie Pl

Dean Tce

13 🔒
8

5 ✕ ⊙ 2
India Pl

Floatarium Spa

STOCKBRIDGE

Ann St

Water of Leith

S Learmonth Gdns

Doune Tce

Gloucester La

India St

Heriot Row

Buckingham Tce

Eton Tce

Dean Gardens

Moray Pl

Belgrave Cres

Sights

Glenogle Swim Centre
SWIMMING

1 Map p106, C2

Atmospheric Victorian swimming baths with a 25m pool, sauna and gym. (☎343 6376; www.edinburghleisure.co.uk; Glenogle Rd; adult/child £4.20/2.10; �7am-10pm Mon Fri, 8am-4pm Sat & Sun; ☐36)

Floatarium Spa
HEALTH & FITNESS

2 Map p106, D4

Escape from the bustle of the city centre in a warm, womb-like flotation tank, or enjoy the many other therapies on offer, including facials, aromatherapy massage, reflexology, shiatsu, reiki and Indian head massage (appointments necessary). There's a sweet-scented shop, too, where you can buy massage oils, incense, candles, homeopathic

remedies, CDs and so on. (☎225 3350; edinburghfloatarium.co.uk; 29 NW Circus Pl; float per hr £35; �10am-3pm Mon, to 8pm Tue-Fri, to 6pm Sat, to 5pm Sun; ☐24, 29, 42)

Eating

Buffalo Grill
AMERICAN ££

4 Map p106, C3

This Stockbridge incarnation of Buffalo Grill is a bit more spacious than the original branch in Chapel St, but has the same Wild West decor and beefy, all-American menu. Unlike the original branch this place is fully licensed, but they still allow you to

---

Understand
Water of Leith

Edinburgh's river is a modest stream, flowing only 20 miles from the northwestern slopes of the Pentland Hills to enter the Firth of Forth at Leith. It cuts a surprisingly rural swathe through the city, providing an important wildlife habitat (you can occasionally see otters and kingfishers) and offering the chance to stroll along wooded riverbanks only 500m from Princes St. The Water of Leith Walkway offers an almost uninterrupted 12-mile walking and cycling route along the river from Leith via Stockbridge and Dean Village to Balerno, on the southwestern edge of the city.

BYOB if you prefer (£1 corkage per bottle of wine). (☎332 3864; www. buffalogrill.co.uk; 1 Raeburn Pl; mains £9-19; ⏰6-10.30pm Mon-Thu, to 11pm Fri, 5-11pm Sat, to 10.30pm Sun; 🚌24, 32, 49)

Songkran II

THAI **££**

 5 Map p106, D4

Songkran II dishes up the same menu of excellent Thai food as the West End branch, but in the more romantic atmosphere of a 17th-century town house, decorated with Thai paintings, statues and wood-carvings. (☎225 4804; 8 Gloucester St; ⏰noon-2.30pm & 6-10.45pm Mon-Sat, 6-10.45pm Sun; 🚌24, 29, 42)

Drinking

Stockbridge Tap

PUB

6 Map p106, C3

This cosy bar has more of a lounge atmosphere (sofas at the back) than a traditional Edinburgh pub, but the counter reveals that it is dedicated to real ale – there are seven hand-pulled pints on offer, with three house and four guest beers. There's a good range of boutique gins too. (2 Raeburn Pl; ⏰noon-midnight Mon-Thu, to 1am Fri & Sat, 12.30pm-midnight Sun; 🐾; 🚌24, 29, 42)

Antiquary

PUB

7 Map p106, D4

A dark, downstairs den of traditional beersmanship, with bare wooden floorboards and dark wood tables and chairs, the long-established Antiquary has lively open folk-music sessions on Thursday nights at 9pm, when all comers are welcome to perform. (☎225 2858; www.theantiquarybar.co.uk; 72-78 St Stephen St; ⏰11.30am-11pm Mon, 11.30am-12.30am Tue & Wed, 11.30am-1am Thu-Sat, 12.30pm-12.30am Sun; 🚌24, 29, 42)

Bailie Bar

PUB

8 Map p106, D4

Tucked down in a basement, the Bailie is an old Stockbridge stalwart; a dimly lit, warm and welcoming nook with a large circular island bar, a roaring fire in winter and TVs screening live football. Serves good coffee as well as real ales and malt whiskies. (☎225 4673; thebailiebar.co.uk; 2 St Stephen St; ⏰11am-midnight Mon-Thu, to 1am Fri & Sat, 12.30-11pm Sun; 🚌24, 29, 42)

Shopping

Adam Pottery

HANDICRAFTS

9 Map p106, D3

Produces its own ceramics, mostly decorative, in a wide range of styles. (www.adampottery.co.uk; 76 Henderson Row; ⏰11am-6pm Mon-Sat; 🚌24, 29, 32)

Annie Smith

JEWELLERY

10 Map p106, C3

Annie Smith's back-of-the-shop studio creates beautiful and original contemporary jewellery in silver and 18-carat gold, with beaten and worked surfaces that reflect natural textures such as rock, ice and leaves. If there's nothing in the shop that takes your fancy, you can commission Ms Smith to make something to order. (📞332 5749; www.anniesmith.co.uk; 20 Raeburn Pl; ⏰10am-5.30pm Mon-Sat, noon-5pm Sun, 🚌24, 29, 42)

Bliss
GIFTS

11 🛍 Map p106, C3

This is a great place for girly gifts, from colourful handmade cards and gift wrap to copper and silver jewellery, scented candles, art prints and accessories. (📞332 4605; 5 Raeburn Pl; ⏰10am-5.30pm Mon-Sat, 1-5pm Sun; 🚌24, 29, 42)

Galerie Mirages
JEWELLERY

12 🛍 Map p106, C3

An Aladdin's cave packed with jewellery, textiles and handicrafts from all over the world, best known for its silver, amber and gemstone jewellery in both ethnic and contemporary designs. (www.galeriemirages.co.uk; 46a Raeburn Pl; ⏰10.30am-5.30pm Mon-Sat, 1-5pm Sun; 🚌24, 29, 42)

Ian Mellis
FOOD & DRINK

13 🛍 Map p106, D4

The Stockbridge branch of Scotland's finest cheesemonger purveys the best of British and Irish cheeses. This is the place to purchase traditional Scottish cheeses, from smooth Lanark Blue (the Scottish Roquefort) to sharp Isle of Mull Cheddar. (📞225 6566; www.mellischeese.co.uk; 6 Bakers Pl, Kerr St;

LONELY PLANET/GETTY IMAGES ©

Annie Smith

⏰9.30am-6pm Mon-Wed, to 6.30pm Thu, to 7pm Fri, 9am-6pm Sat, 11am-5pm Sun; 🚌24, 29, 42)

Kiss the Fish
GIFTS

14 🛍 Map p106, B3

This is not just a gift shop, but also an arts and crafts studio where kids can get their hands on stuff to make and decorate. (📞332 8912; www.kissthefishstudios.com; 9 Dean Park St; ⏰10am-5.30pm Mon-Sat, 11am-4.30pm Sun; 🚌24, 29, 42)

Explore

Leith

Leith has been Edinburgh's seaport since the 14th century, but it fell into decay following WWII. It is now undergoing a steady revival, with old warehouses turned into luxury flats and a lush crop of trendy bars and restaurants sprouting up along the waterfront leading to Ocean Terminal, a huge new shopping and leisure complex, and the former Royal Yacht Britannia.

The Sights in a Day

Begin your day with a stroll along **The Shore** (p115; pictured left), Leith's original waterfront. Cross the Water of Leith and follow Ocean Dr to **Ocean Terminal** (p119), where you can spend the rest of the morning aboard the **Royal Yacht Britannia** (p112); don't forget to take tea and scones in the ship's Royal Deck Tea Room.

There are plenty of good lunch spots with outdoor tables at nearby Victoria Dock. **A Room in Leith** (p117) has tables on a pontoon floating in the dock, while you'll need to reserve well ahead to get a table at Michelin-starred **The Kitchin** (p116) In the afternoon, head west to **Newhaven Harbour** (p115) for a wildlife boat trip around the islands in the Firth of Forth.

Leith nightlife is more about eating and drinking than culture and entertainment, so – once again plan in advance to be sure of a dinner table at one of the neighbourhood's top restaurants: **Martin Wishart** (p116) or **Plumed Horse** (p116). Follow up with cocktails served in a teapot at the **Roseleaf** (p117), or pints of real ale at **Teuchters Landing** (p118).

👁 Top Sights
Royal Yacht Britannia (p112)

❤ Best of Edinburgh

Eating
Fishers Bistro (p116)
Martin Wishart (p116)
The Kitchin (p116)
Plumed Horse (p116)
Shore (p117)

Shopping
Kinloch Anderson (p119)

Getting There

🚌 **Bus** Lothian Buses 10, 12, 16 and 22 run from Princes St down Leith Walk to the junction of Constitution and Great Junction Sts; from here 10 and 16 go west to Newhaven; 22 goes north to The Shore and Ocean Terminal. Buses 11, 34, 35 and 36 also terminate at Ocean Terminal.

Top Sights
Royal Yacht Britannia

Built on Clydeside, the former Royal Yacht Britannia was the British royal family's floating holiday home during their foreign travels from the time of her launch in 1953 until her decommissioning in 1997, and is now moored permanently in front of Ocean Terminal. The tour gives an intriguing insight into the queen's private tastes – the ship is a monument to 1950s decor, and the accommodation reveals Her Majesty's preference for simple, unfussy surroundings.

 Map p114, A1

www.royalyachtbritannia.co.uk

Ocean Terminal

adult/child £12/7.50

🕑9.30am-6pm Jul-Sep, to 5.30pm Apr-Jun & Oct, 10am-5pm Nov-Mar

Staircase of the Royal Yacht Britannia

Don't Miss

State Apartments

The queen travelled with 45 members of the royal household, five tons of luggage and a Rolls-Royce that was squeezed into a specially built garage on the deck (it's still there). The **State Drawing Room**, which once hosted royal receptions, is furnished with chintz sofas bolted firmly to the floor, and a baby grand piano where Noel Coward once tickled the ivories.

Royal Bedrooms

The private cabins of the queen and Prince Philip are surprisingly small and plain, with ordinary 3ft-wide single beds (the only double bed on board is in the honeymoon suite, used by Prince Charles and Lady Diana in 1981). The thermometer in the queen's bathroom was used to make sure the water was the correct temperature, and when in harbour one yachtsman was charged with ensuring that the angle of the gangway never exceeded 12 degrees.

On Deck

The decks (of Burmese teak) were scrubbed daily, but all work near the royal accommodation was carried out in complete silence and had to be finished by 8am. Note the mahogany windbreak that was added to the balcony deck in front of the bridge. It was put there to stop wayward breezes from blowing up skirts and inadvertently revealing the royal undies.

Bloodhound

Britannia was joined in 2010 by the 1930s racing yacht *Bloodhound*, which was owned by the queen in the 1960s. She is moored alongside Britannia (except in July and August, when she is away cruising) as part of an exhibition about the royal family's love of all things nautical.

☑ Top Tips

▶ You tour the ship at your own pace, using an audioguide. You'll need at least two hours to see everything.

▶ The Majestic Tour (p152) bus runs from Waverley Bridge to Britannia during opening times.

▶ Last admission is 90 minutes before closing.

▶ The **Royal Edinburgh Ticket** (adult/child £45/25), available from Majestic Tour, gives admission to Britannia, Edinburgh Castle and the Palace of Holyroodhouse, plus two days travel on local tour buses.

✗ Take a Break

Britannia's sun deck (now enclosed in glass) makes a stunning setting for the **Royal Deck Tea Room** (mains £5-13; ⏰10am-4.30pm Apr-Oct, 10.30am-4pm Nov-Mar), where you can enjoy coffee and cake, or even a bottle of champagne, with a view across the Firth of Forth to the hills of Fife.

A | B | C | D

Western Harbour

Royal Yacht Britannia ◉

Leith Docks

Imperial Dock

N 0 — 200 m
0 — 0.1 miles

For reviews see

◉ Top Sights — p112
◉ Sights — p115
✖ Eating — p116
🍷 Drinking — p117
🔒 Shopping — p119

🔒 20

Ocean Dr

Victoria Dock

Albert Dock

Victoria Quay

◀◉ 1

Commercial Quay

Tower Pl

Commercial St

🍷 16 🍷 17

✖ 10

Dock Pl

✖ 5 Tower St

The Shore ◉ 3 Tower St

✖ 7

🔒 19 Dock St

✖ 9

N Junction St

Coburg St

Sandport Pl

✖ 12

Bernard St

Water of Leith

13 🔒

18

✖ 6 The Shore

Baltic St

Mill La

Water St

🍷 15

✖ 11

14 🍷

Tolbooth Wynd

Maritime St

Mitchell St

Bangor Rd

Great Junction St

Cables Wynd

Henderson St

🔒 8

Giles St

Kirkgate

Constitution St

Queen Charlotte St

John's Pl

Poplar La

Links Pl

Elbe St

Bonnington Rd

Jane St

Tennant St

4 ◉ Trinity House

Wellington Pl

Duncan Pl

Leith Links

Pilrig Park

Duke St

2 ◉ Leith Links

Sights

Newhaven Harbour
HARBOUR

1 ◎ Map p114, A2

Newhaven was once a distinctive fishing community whose fishwives tramped the streets of Edinburgh's New Town selling *caller herrin* (fresh herring) from wicker creels on their backs. Modern development has dispelled the fishing-village atmosphere, but the little harbour still boasts a picturesque lighthouse. **Sea.fari** (☎331 4857; www.seafari.co.uk; adult/child £22/19; ☐7, 11, 16) offers one-hour boat trips from the harbour to see seals and seabirds (advance booking essential). (Newhaven Pl; ☐7, 11,16)

Leith Links
PARK

2 ◎ Map p114, D5

This public park was originally common grazing land, but is more famous as the birthplace of modern golf. Although St Andrews has the oldest golf course in the world, it was at Leith Links in 1744 that the first official rules of the game were formulated by the Honorable Company of Edinburgh Golfers. (☐12, 21, 25, 34, 49)

The Shore
STREET

3 ◎ Map p114, C3

The most attractive part of Leith is this cobbled waterfront street lined with pubs and restaurants. Before the docks were built in the 19th century this was Leith's original wharf. An iron plaque in front of No 30 marks the King's Landing – the spot where King George IV (the first reigning British monarch to visit Scotland since Charles II in 1650) stepped ashore in 1822. (☐16, 22, 35, 36)

Trinity House
MUSEUM

4 ◎ Map p114, C4

This neoclassical building dating from 1816 was the headquarters of the Incorporation of Masters and Mariners (founded in 1380), the nautical equivalent of a tradesmen's guild, and is a treasurehouse of old ship models, navigation instruments and nautical memorabilia relating to Leith's

The Shore

Ⓠ Local Life
Cramond Village

With its moored yachts, stately swans and whitewashed houses spilling down the hillside at the mouth of the River Almond, Cramond (4 miles west of Leith) is the most picturesque corner of Edinburgh. Originally a mill village, it has a historic 17th-century church and 15th-century tower house, as well as some rather unimpressive Roman remains, but most people come to stroll along the seafront, have a drink in the local pub, and enjoy the walks along the river to the ruined mills.

maritime history. Admission is by pre-booked one-hour guided tour only. (📞554 3289; www.trinityhouseleith.org.uk; 99 Kirkgate; adult/child £4.50/2.70; ⏰9.30am-4.30pm Mon-Fri; 🚌all Leith Walk buses)

Eating

Fishers Bistro   SEAFOOD ££

5 🍴 Map p114, C2

This cosy little restaurant, tucked beneath a 17th-century signal tower, is one of the city's best seafood places. The menu ranges widely, from classic fishcakes with lemon and chive mayonnaise, and sea bass with crispy capers, to more exotic delights such as razor clams with chorizo, and queenie scallops with dill and fennel butter. (📞554 5666; www.fishersbistros.co.uk; 1 The Shore; mains £10-19; ⏰noon-10.30pm; 📶🅿♿; 🚌16, 22, 35, 36)

Martin Wishart   FRENCH £££

6 🍴 Map p114, C3

In 2001 this restaurant became the first in Edinburgh to win a Michelin star. The eponymous chef has worked with Albert Roux, Marco Pierre White and Nick Nairn, and brings a modern French approach to the best Scottish produce, from roast scallop with puy lentils and chopped pig's trotter, to roast shoulder of beef with morels and bordelaise sauce. (📞553 3557; www.martin-wishart.co.uk; 54 The Shore; 3-course lunch/dinner £29/70; ⏰lunch & dinner Tue-Sat; 🅿; 🚌16, 22, 35, 36)

The Kitchin   SCOTTISH £££

7 🍴 Map p114, B3

Fresh, seasonal, locally sourced Scottish produce is the philosophy that has won a Michelin star for this elegant but unpretentious restaurant. The menu moves with the seasons, of course, so expect fresh salads in summer and game in winter, and shellfish dishes when there's an 'r' in the month. Three-course lunch menu £26.50. (📞555 1755; www.thekitchin.com; 78 Commercial Quay; mains £33-35; ⏰lunch & dinner Tue-Sat; 🅿; 🚌16, 22, 35, 36)

Plumed Horse   SCOTTISH £££

8 🍴 Map p114, B4

Smartly suited and booted staff welcome you to this quiet corner of understated elegance, where the muted decor of pale blues and greens, cream leather chairs and crisp white linen places the focus firmly on the exquisitely prepared and presented food – fresh Scottish produce with a slight French accent. Eight-course tasting menu £69, plus £48 for matching wines. (📞554 5556; www.plumedhorse. co.uk; 50-54 Henderson St; 3-course dinner £55; ⏰lunch & dinner Tue-Sat)

Shore
SEAFOOD ££

9 🍴 Map p114, C3

The atmospheric dining room next door to the popular Shore pub is a haven of wood-panelled peace, with old photographs, nautical knick-knacks, fresh flowers and an open fire adding to the romantic theme. The menu changes daily and specialises in Scottish seafood and game, with an all day bar menu that includes haddock and chips and seafood pie. (📞553 5080; 3-4 The Shore; mains £10-20; ⏰noon-10.30pm; 🛜💺; 🚌16, 22, 35, 36)

A Room in Leith
SCOTTISH ££

10 🍴 Map p114, C2

This restaurant (and its companion bar, Teuchters Landing) inhabits a warren of nooks and crannies in a red-brick building (once a waiting room for ferries across the Firth of Forth). The Scottish-flavoured menu includes haggis with mustard-and-cider cream sauce, and roast pork with caramelised root vegetables. (📞554 7427; www.aroomin.co.uk; 1c Dock Pl; mains £11-17; ⏰lunch & dinner; 🛜💺; 🚌16, 22, 35, 36)

Café Truva
CAFE £

11 🍴 Map p114, C3

A firm favourite with local Leithers, Truva combines a standard cafe menu of breakfast fry-ups, coffee, soups and sandwiches with a tempting array of Turkish specialities, from roast aubergines and tomatoes to hummus or sweet, sticky baklava. (📞556 9524; 77 The Shore; mains £6-10; ⏰8am-6pm; 📞; 🚌16, 22, 35, 36)

Diner 7
STEAKHOUSE £

12 🍴 Map p114, C3

A neat local eatery with rust-coloured leather booths and banquettes, black and copper tables, and local art on the walls, this diner has a menu of succulent Aberdeen Angus steaks and homemade burgers, but also offers more unusual fare such as chicken and chorizo kebabs, or smoked haddock with black-pudding stovies (stewed potatoes). (www.diner7.co.uk; 7 Commercial St; mains £7-12; ⏰4-11pm Mon-Sat, 11am-11pm Sun; 🚌16, 22, 35, 36)

Drinking

Roseleaf
CAFE-BAR

13 🍷 Map p114, B3

Cute and quaint, the Roseleaf could hardly be further from the average Leith bar. It's decked out in flowered wallpaper, old furniture and rose-patterned china (cocktails are served in teapots); the real ales and bottled

Top Tip

Top 5 Edinburgh Novels

▶ *The Prime of Miss Jean Brodie* (Muriel Spark, 1962) The story of a charismatic teacher in a 1930s Edinburgh girls school.

▶ *Trainspotting* (Irvine Welsh, 1993) A disturbing and darkly humorous journey through the junkie underworld of 1990s Edinburgh.

▶ *Complicity* (Iain Banks, 1993) Gruesome and often hilarious thriller-cum-satire on the greed and corruption of the Thatcher years.

▶ *Born Free* (Laura Hird, 1999) A gritty and tragic but heart-warming tale of modern family life in one of Edinburgh's poorer neighbourhoods.

▶ *The Falls* by Ian Rankin (2001) A gripping noir-style crime novel that stars hard-drinking detective John Rebus, Edinburgh's answer to Sam Spade.

beers are complemented by a range of speciality teas, coffees and fruit drinks (including rose lemonade) and above-average pub grub (served 10am to 10pm). (☏476 5268; www.roseleaf.co.uk; 23-24 Sandport Pl; ☺10am-1am; 🛜👶; 🚌16, 22, 35, 36)

Teuchters Landing   PUB

The award-winning bar at A Room in Leith restaurant (see 10 🍴 Map p114, C2)

is famed for its range of real ales (no fewer than 18 on tap) and malt whiskies (more than 90 varieties) which you can enjoy at outdoor tables on a floating terrace in the dock. (www.aroomin.co.uk; 1 Dock Pl; 🛜; 🚌16, 22, 35 or 36)

Sofi's   BAR

14 🍺 Map p114, B4

Sofi's brings a little bit of Swedish sophistication to this former Leith pub, feeling more like a bohemian cafe with its mismatched furniture, candlelit tables, fresh flowers and colourful art. It's a real community place too, hosting film screenings, book clubs, open-mic music nights, and even a knitting club. (☏555 7019; www.bodabar.com; 65 Henderson St; 🛜; 🚌22, 36)

Port O'Leith   PUB

15 🍺 Map p114, D3

This is a good, old-fashioned, friendly local boozer, swathed with flags and cap bands left behind by visiting sailors – Leith docks are just down the road. Pop in for a pint and you'll probably stay until closing time. (www.portoleithpub.com; 58 Constitution St; 🚌16, 22, 35 or 36)

Starbank Inn   PUB

16 🍺 Map p114, A2

The Starbank is an oasis of fine ales and good, homemade food on Edinburgh's windswept waterfront. In summer there's a sunny conservatory, and

in winter a blazing fire. (www.starbankinn
-edinburgh.co.uk; 64 Laverockbank Rd)

Old Chain Pier PUB

17 🚇 Map p114, A2

Recently renovated, the delightful
Old Chain Pier is a real-ale pub full
of polished wood, brass and nautical
paraphernalia, and with a brilliant
location overlooking the sea. The
building was once the 19th-century
booking office for steamers across the
Firth of Forth (the pier from which it
takes its name was washed away in a
storm in 1898). (📞552 1233; old-chain
-pier.co.uk; 32 Trinity Cres; 🚌16)

LONELY PLANET/GETTY IMAGES ©

Old Chain Pier

Shopping

Flux ARTS & CRAFTS

18 🛍 Map p114, C3

Flux is an outlet for contemporary
British and overseas arts and crafts,
including stained glass, metalware,
jewellery and ceramics, all ethically
sourced and many made using recy-
cled materials. (📞554 4075; www.get2flux.
co.uk; 55 Bernard St; 🕙11am-6pm Mon-Sat,
noon-5pm Sun; 🚌16, 22, 35, 36)

Kinloch Anderson FASHION

19 🛍 Map p114, B3

One of the best kilt shops in town,
Kinloch Anderson was founded in
1868 and is still family-run. The company has a royal warrant, meaning
it is an official supplier of kilts and
Highland dress to the royal family.
(www.kinlochanderson.com; 4 Dock St; 🚌16,
22, 35, 36)

Ocean Terminal MALL

20 🛍 Map p114, A1

Anchored by Debenhams and BHS
department stores, Ocean Terminal
is the biggest shopping centre in
Edinburgh; fashion outlets include
Fat Face, GAP, Schuh, Superdry
and White Stuff. (📞555 8888; www.
oceanterminal.com; Ocean Dr; 🕙10am-8pm
Mon-Fri, to 7pm Sat, 11am-6pm Sun; 🚌11, 22,
34, 35, 36)

Explore

South Edinburgh

Stretching south from the Old Town and taking in the 19th-century tenements of Tollcross, Bruntsfield and Marchmont, and the upmarket suburbs of Newington, Grange and Morningside, this is a peaceful residential neighbourhood of smart Victorian flats and spacious garden villas. There's not much to see in the way of tourist attractions, but there are many good restaurants, cafes and pubs.

The Sights in a Day

☀ Start the day with breakfast at **Peter's Yard** (p126), then enjoy a leisurely stroll through **the Meadows** (p124) – look to see if there's a cricket match in progress – and spend the rest of the morning browsing the exhibits at the **Surgeons' Hall Museums** (p124; pictured left) before sitting down to a lunch of Indian 'tapas' at **Mother India's Cafe** (p126).

☀ In the afternoon, take a bus to **Blackford Hill** (p124), and spend an hour or two exploring the walking trails here and in the neighbouring **Hermitage of Braid** (p124), and climb to the summit of the hill for a glorious late-afternoon view across the city to the castle, the Old Town skyline and Arthur's Seat.

🌙 Book well in advance to be sure of a table at **Timberyard** (p125), and check the listings to see if there's a show on at the **Festival Theatre** (p128). If it's a sunny summer evening you might prefer to indulge in outdoor drinks at **Pear Tree House** (p127).

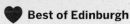 **Best of Edinburgh**

Drinking
Bennet's Bar (p127)
Blue Blazer (p127)

Eating
Timberyard (p125)
Kalpna (p127)

Shopping
Word Power (p129)

Museums & Galleries
Surgeons' Hall Museums (p124)

Getting There

🚌 **Bus** The main bus routes south from the city centre are 10, 11, 15, 16, 17, 23, 27 and 45 from the west end of Princes St to Tollcross (all except 10 and 27 continue south to Bruntsfield and Morningside); and 3, 5, 7, 8, 29, 31, 37, 47 and 49 from North Bridge to Newington.

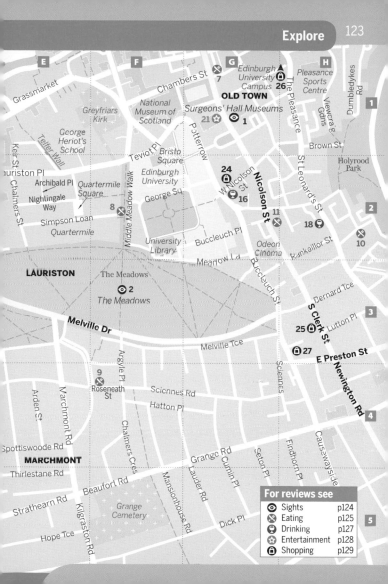

E Grassmarket

F Chambers St

G ✪ 7
Edinburgh University Campus 26
The Pleasance

H Pleasance Sports Centre
Dumbledykes Rd
Viewcrag Gdns

OLD TOWN

Greyfriars Kirk

National Museum of Scotland

Surgeons' Hall Museums
21 ✪   ◉ 1

Brown St
Holyrood Park

George Heriot's School

Teviot Pl   Bristo Square

Potterrow

24 ◉

Keir St
Telfer Wall

Lauriston Pl
Archibald Pl
Nightingale Way

Chalmers St

Quartermile Square

Edinburgh University

George Sq

W Nicolson St

16 ◉

Nicolson St

11 ✪

18 ◉

St Leonard's St

Viewcraig Gdns

1

2

10 ✪

8 ✪

Simpson Loan
Quartermile

University Library

Buccleuch Pl

Meadow La

Odeon Cinema

Buccleuch St

Rankeillor St

LAURISTON

The Meadows
◉ 2
The Meadows

Bernard Tce

S Clerk St

Lutton Pl

25 ✪

Melville Dr

Melville Tce

◉ 27

E Preston St

Newington Rd

9 ✪
Roseneath St

Argyle Pl

Sciennes Rd

Hatton Pl

Sciennes

Arden St

Marchmont Rd

Chalmers Cres

Causewayside

Findhorn Pl

3

4

Spottiswoode Rd

MARCHMONT

Thirlestane Rd

Beaufort Rd

Grange Rd

Cumin Pl

Seton Pl

Mansionhouse Rd

Lauder Rd

Strathearn Rd

Kilgraston Rd

Grange Cemetery

Dick Pl

Hope Tce

5

Sights

Surgeons' Hall Museums
MUSEUM

1 ⊙ Map p122, G1

Housed in a grand Ionic temple designed by William Playfair in 1832, this museum provides a fascinating look at surgery in Scotland from the 15th century – when barbers supplemented their income with bloodletting and amputations – to the present day. The highlight is the grisly exhibit on the bodysnatchers Burke and Hare, which includes Burke's death mask and a pocketbook bound in his skin. (www.museum.rcsed.ac.uk; Nicolson St; adult/child £5/3; ⊙10am-5pm daily Apr-Oct, noon-4pm Mon-Fri Nov-Mar; ◻all South Bridge buses)

The Meadows
PARK

2 ⊙ Map p122, F3

This mile-long stretch of lush grass criss-crossed with tree-lined walks was once a shallow lake known as the Borough Loch. Drained in the 1740s and converted into parkland, it's a great place for a picnic or a quiet stroll – in springtime its walks lie ankle-deep in drifts of pink cherry blossom, and there are great views of Arthur's Seat. (Melville Dr; ◻all Tollcross, South Bridge buses)

Blackford Hill
VIEWPOINT

3 ⊙ Map p122, D5

A patch of countryside enclosed by the city's southern suburbs, craggy Blackford Hill (164m) offers pleasant walking and splendid views. The panorama to the north takes in Edinburgh Castle atop its rock, the bristling spine of the Old Town, the monuments on Calton Hill and the 'sleeping lion' of Arthur's Seat. (Charterhall Rd; ◻24, 38, 41)

Hermitage of Braid
WILDLIFE RESERVE

4 ⊙ Map p122, B5

The Hermitage of Braid is a wooded valley criss-crossed with walking trails to the south of Blackford Hill – with sunlight filtering through the leaves and the sound of birdsong all around, you'll feel miles from the city here. **Hermitage House** (admission free; ⊙9am-4pm Mon-Fri, noon-4pm Sun, closed

The Meadows

Sat), an 18th-century mansion, houses a visitor centre that explains the history and wildlife of the glen, and has details of nearby nature trails. (www. fohb.org; 📖 5, 11, 15, 16)

Eating

Timberyard   SCOTTISH ££

5 🍴 Map p122, D1

Ancient floorboards, cast-iron pillars, exposed joists and tables made from slabs of old mahogany create a rustic, retro atmosphere in this slow-food restaurant where the accent is on locally sourced produce from artisan growers and foragers. Typical dishes include seared scallop with apple,

jerusalem artichoke and sorrel; and juniper-smoked pigeon with wild garlic flowers and beetroot. (📞 221 1222; www.timberyard.co; 10 Lady Lawson St; mains £17-20; 🕑 lunch & dinner Tue-Sat; 🛜; 📖 2, 35)

Leven's   FUSION ££

6 🍴 Map p122, D3

From the spectacular modern chandeliers and slowly pulsing blue/purple mood lighting to the designer colour palette and Villeroy & Boch tableware, everything about this restaurant oozes style. The food lives up to the surroundings, with clever and unexpected combinations of flavours, colours and textures in dishes such as beef sirloin Panang curry, with peanuts and lime

Local Life
Southside Brunch

One of South Edinburgh's favourite places to kick back over brunch with the weekend papers, **Loudon's** (Map p122, C2; www.loudons-cafe.co.uk; 94b Fountainbridge; mains £3-7; ⏰8am-6pm Mon-Fri, 9am-6pm Sat & Sun; 🔊👶; 🚌1, 34, 35) is a cafe that bakes its own organic bread, serves ethically sourced coffee, and has an all-day brunch menu (ends at 3pm Saturday and Sunday) that includes eggs Benedict, warm spiced quinoa with dried fruit, and specials such as blueberry pancakes with fruit salad.

leaves. (📞229 8988; 30-32 Leven St; mains £12-20; ⏰lunch & dinner Sun-Thu, noon-10.30pm Fri & Sat; 🚌11, 15, 16, 23, 45)

Mother India's Cafe INDIAN ££

7 🍴 Map p122, G1

A simple concept pioneered in Glasgow has captured hearts and minds – and stomachs – in Edinburgh: Indian food served in tapas-size portions, so that you can sample a greater variety of different dishes without busting your gut. Hugely popular, so book a table to avoid disappointment. (📞524 9801; www.motherindia.co.uk; 3-5 Infirmary St; tapas £4-6; ⏰lunch & dinner Mon-Thu, noon-10pm Fri-Sun; 🚌all South Bridge buses)

Peter's Yard CAFE £

8 🍴 Map p122, F2

This Swedish-style coffee house produces its own homebaked breads, from sourdough to focaccia, which form the basis for lunchtime sandwiches with fillings such as roast beef with beetroot and caper salad, and roast butternut squash with sunblush tomato pesto. Breakfast (served till noon) can be a basket of breads with conserves and cheeses, or yogurt with granola and fruit. (www.petersyard.com; 27 Simpson Loan; mains £5-8; ⏰7.30am-8pm Mon, to 10pm Tue-Fri, 9am-10pm Sat & Sun; 🚌23, 27, 35, 45, 47)

Sweet Melindas SCOTTISH £££

9 🍴 Map p122, F4

With ingredients sourced from the fishmonger next door and the vegetable market around the corner, and everything from the bread to the chocolate truffles handmade in the kitchen, Sweet Melindas offers a true taste of Scottish home cooking. The ambience is chilled and the menu concentrates on seafood and game, with at least one vegetarian starter and main. (📞229 7953; www.sweetmelindas.co.uk; 11 Roseneath St; ⏰lunch & dinner Tue-Sat; 🔊👶; 🚌24, 41)

Engine Shed VEGETARIAN £

10 🍴 Map p122, H2

This fair-trade, organic vegetarian cafe is an ideal spot for a healthy lunch, or a cuppa and a bakery-fresh scone after climbing Arthur's Seat. It's been set up to provide employment and training for special-needs adults, and as well as having its own bakery it also makes its own tofu, which is used plentifully in its tasty curries. (www.theengineshed.org; 19 St Leonard's Lane; mains £4-7; ⏰10am-4pm Mon-Sat; 🔊♿👶; 🚌14)

Kalpna   INDIAN ££

11 🍴 Map p122, G2

A long-standing Edinburgh favourite, Kalpna is one of the best Indian restaurants in the country, vegetarian or otherwise. The cuisine is mostly Gujarati, with a smattering of dishes from other parts of India. The all-you-can-eat lunch buffet (£8) is superb value. (📞667 9890; www.kalpnarestaurant.com; 2-3 St Patrick Sq; mains £6-11; ⏲lunch & dinner Mon-Sat year-round, plus dinner Sun May-Sep; 🖋; 🚌all Newington buses)

Katie's Diner   AMERICAN ££

12 🍴 Map p122, C3

As you might expect from a place run by a husband-and-wife team, this cute little diner has a warm welcome and a homely atmosphere. The handful of tables enjoy a view onto the parkland of Bruntsfield Links, and the menu runs from barbecue chicken wings and nachos to prime Scottish steaks and juicy homemade burgers with fries and coleslaw. (📞229 1394; www.katiesdiner.com; 12 Barclay Tce; mains £9-24; ⏲6-9pm Tue-Thu, to 9.30pm Fri & Sat; 🚌all Bruntsfield buses)

Drinking

Bennet's Bar   PUB

13 🍺 Map p122, D3

One of Edinburgh's most famous pubs, Bennet's has managed to hang on to almost all of its beautiful Victorian fittings, from the leaded stained-glass windows and ornate mirrors to the wooden gantry and the brass water taps on the bar (for your whisky – there are over 100 malts from which to choose). (www.bennetsbar.co.uk; 8 Leven St; 🚌all Tollcross buses)

Blue Blazer   PUB

14 🍺 Map p122, D1

With its bare wooden floors, cosy fireplace and efficient bar staff, the Blue Blazer is a down-to-earth antidote to the designer excess of modern style bars, catering to a loyal clientele of real-ale enthusiasts, pie eaters and Saturday horse-racing fans. (📞229 5030; 2 Spittal St; 🍴; 🚌2 or 35)

Canny Man's   PUB

15 🍺 Map p122, C5

A lovely eccentric pub, the Canny Man's is a crowded warren of tiny rooms crammed with a bizarre collection of antiques and curiosities, where the landlord regularly refuses entry to anyone who looks scruffy, inebriated or vaguely pinko/commie/subversive. If you can get in, you'll find it serves excellent real ale, superb Bloody Marys, vintage port and Cuban cigars. (📞447 1484; 237 Morningside Rd; 📶; 🚌11, 15, 16, 17, 23)

Pear Tree House   PUB

16 🍺 Map p122, G2

Set in an 18th-century house with cobbled courtyard, the Pear Tree is a student favourite with an open fire in winter, comfy sofas and board games inside, plus the city's biggest and most popular beer garden in summer. (www.pear-tree-house.co.uk; 38 West Nicolson St; 🛜; 🚌2, 41, 42, 47)

Athletic Arms

PUB

17 🚇 Map p122, A3

Nicknamed Diggers, after the cemetery across the street (the grave-diggers used to nip in and slake their thirst), this pub dates from the 1890s and is still staunchly traditional. It has a reputation as a real-ale drinker's mecca, serving locally brewed Diggers' 80-shilling ale, and is packed to the gills with football and rugby fans on match days. (1-3 Angle Park Tce; 🚌1, 34, 35)

Auld Hoose

PUB

18 🚇 Map p122, H2

Promoting itself as the Southside's only 'alternative' pub, the Auld Hoose certainly lives up to its reputation with unpretentious, old-fashioned decor, a range of real ales from Scottish microbreweries (Trashy Blonde from BrewDog, Avalanche Ale from Loch Fyne in Argyll), and a jukebox that would make the late John Peel weep with joy. (📞668 2934; www.theauldhoose.co.uk; 23-25 St Leonards St; 🛜; 🚌14)

Brauhaus

BAR

19 🚇 Map p122, D2

The bar may be small – half a dozen bar stools, a couple of sofas and a scattering of seats – but its ambition is huge, with a vast menu of bottled beers from all over the world, ranging from the usual Belgian, German and Czech suspects to more unusual brews such as Paradox Smokehead (a 10% ABV stout aged for six months in a whisky cask). (📞656 0356; 105 Lauriston Pl; 🕐noon-1am; 🚌23, 27, 35, 45)

Entertainment

Cameo

CINEMA

20 ⭐ Map p122, C2

The three-screen, independently owned Cameo is a good, old-fashioned cinema showing an imaginative mix of mainstream and art-house movies. There is a good program of midnight movies and Sunday matinees, and the seats in screen 1 are big enough to get lost in. (www.picturehouses.co.uk; 38 Home St; 🚌all Tollcross buses)

Edinburgh Festival Theatre

DANCE, OPERA

21 ⭐ Map p122, G1

A beautifully restored art deco theatre, the Festival is the city's main venue for opera, dance and ballet, but also stages musicals, concerts, drama and children's shows. (www.edtheatres.com/festival; 13-29 Nicolson St; 🕐box office 10am-6pm Mon-Sat, to 8pm show nights, 4pm-showtime Sun; 🚌all South Bridge buses)

King's Theatre

THEATRE

22 ⭐ Map p122, D3

King's is a traditional theatre with a program of musicals, drama, comedy and its famous Christmas panto-mimes. (www.edtheatres.com/kings; 2 Leven St; ☉box office open 1hr before show; 🚌all Tollcross buses)

Wee Red Bar CLUB

23 ⭐ Map p122, D2

The Wee Red Bar has been around so long there's a danger the authorities will slap a blue plaque on it and de-clare it a national monument. Wee, red and frequented by lots of art students, it's famous for the Egg, a weekly smor-gasbord of classic punk, ska, northern soul, indie etc that is still one of the best club nights in the city. (☎651 5859; www.weeredbar.co.uk; Edinburgh College of Art, 74 Lauriston Pl; 🚌23, 27, 35, 45)

Shopping

Word Power BOOKS

24 🔒 Map p122, G2

A radical, independent bookshop with a wide range of political, gay and feminist literature. (www.word-power. co.uk; 43 West Nicolson St; ☉10am-6pm Mon-Sat, noon 5pm Sun; 🚌41, 42)

Hog's Head MUSIC

25 🔒 Map p122, H3

A classic, old-school music and film shop that buys and sells secondhand CDs and DVDs. Thousands of discs and box sets to browse among, a good range of T-shirts, and staff who know whereof they speak. (☎667 5274; www.hogs-head.

Bennet's Bar (p127)

com; 62 South Clerk St; ☉10am-5.30pm Mon-Sat, 12.30-4.30pm Sun; 🚌all Newington buses)

Kilberry Bagpipes MUSIC

26 🔒 Map p122, H1

Makers and retailers of traditional Highland bagpipes, Kilberry also sells piping accessories, snare drums, books, CDs and learning materials. (☎556 9607; www.kilberry.com; 27 St Mary's St; ☉9am-5pm Mon-Fri, to 1pm Sat; 🚌35, 36)

Meadows Pottery HANDICRAFTS

27 🔒 Map p122, H3

Sells colourful stoneware, all hand-thrown on the premises. (www. themeadowspottery.com; 11a Summerhall Pl; ☉10.30am-5pm Mon-Sat; 🚌2, 41, 42, 47)

Top Sights
Rosslyn Chapel

Getting There

🚌 Lothian Buses No 15 (not 15A) runs from the west end of Princes St in Edinburgh, to Roslin village (£1.40, 30 minutes, every 30 minutes), near the chapel.

The success of Dan Brown's novel *The Da Vinci Code* and the subsequent Hollywood film have seen a flood of visitors descend on Scotland's most beautiful and enigmatic church (which features in the novel's finale). Rosslyn Chapel (formally known as the Collegiate Church of St Matthew) was built in the mid-15th century for William St Clair, third earl of Orkney, and the ornately carved interior – at odds with the architectural fashion of its time – is a monument to the mason's art, rich in symbolic imagery and shrouded in mystery.

Don't Miss

The Apprentice Pillar
Perhaps the most beautiful carving in the chapel, at the entrance to the Lady Chapel. Four vines spiral around the pillar, issuing from the mouths of eight dragons at its base. At the top is an image of Isaac, son of Abraham, upon the altar.

Lucifer, the Fallen Angel
At head height in the Lady Chapel, to the left of the second window from left, is an upside-down angel bound with rope, a symbol often associated with freemasonry. The arch above is decorated with the Dance of Death.

The Green Man
On the boss at the base of the arch, between the second and third windows from the left in the Lady Chapel. This is the finest example of more than 100 carvings of the 'green man', a pagan symbol of spring, fertility and rebirth.

Indian Corn
The frieze around the second window in the south wall. It's said to represent Indian corn (maize), but it predates Columbus' discovery of the New World in 1492. Other carvings resemble aloe vera, also American in origin.

The Apprentice
High in the southwest corner, beneath an empty statue niche, is the head of the murdered Apprentice; there's a deep wound in his forehead, above the right eye. The head on the side wall to the left is his mother.

The Ceiling
The spectacular ceiling vault is decorated with engraved roses, lilies and stars.

Chapel Loan, Roslin

www.rosslynchapel.org.uk

adult/child £9/free

⏱ 9.30am-5pm Mon-Sat, noon-4.45pm Sun

☑ Top Tips
▶ Get your tickets in advance through the chapel's website (except in August, when no bookings are taken). No photography allowed inside the chapel.

▶ It's worth buying the official guidebook, finding a bench in the gardens and having a skim through before going into the chapel – the background information will make your visit all the more interesting.

✗ Take a Break
There's a **coffee shop** (mains £5-6; ⏱ 10am-5pm Mon-Sat, noon-4pm Sun) in the chapel's visitor centre, serving soup, sandwiches, coffee and cake, with a view over Roslin Glen.

The Best of
Edinburgh

Edinburgh's Best Walks

Edinburgh's Best...

Scottish National Gallery (p76)
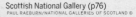

Best Walks
From Castle to Palace

The Walk

Edinburgh Castle, the Palace of Holyroodhouse and the Scottish parliament are what make Edinburgh Scotland's capital. This walk links the city's most iconic sights by following (mostly) the Royal Mile, the ancient processional route followed by kings and queens travelling between castle and palace. Our route occasionally shifts sideways to explore the narrow closes and wynds that lend Edinburgh's Old Town its unique, historic atmosphere.

Start Edinburgh Castle

Finish Palace of Holyroodhouse

Length 1.5 miles; one hour

Take a Break

Victoria St and the Grassmarket, a few minutes walk south of the Royal Mile, are crammed with places to eat. Further down the Royal Mile, Wedgwood (p44) offers fine dining Scottish style .

LONELY PLANET/GETTY IMAGES IMAGES ©

Scottish Parliament Building

❶ Edinburgh Castle

Dominating the city from its superb defensive position, **Edinburgh Castle** (p24) is one of Britain's most impressive fortresses. Check out the Scottish Crown Jewels and wander through the former prisons in the Castle Vaults.

❷ Scotch Whisky Experience

After enjoying the views from the **Castle Esplanade**, head down the Royal Mile. On the left you'll pass the **Witches Well** (a fountain commemorating those executed on suspicion of witchcraft) before reaching the **Scotch Whisky Experience** (p40).

❸ Writers' Museum

Descend Ramsay Lane to the twin towers of Edinburgh's **New College**, and take a peek in the courtyard to see the **statue of John Knox**. Return to the Royal Mile via **Lady Stair's Close**, a picturesque Old Town alley, and the **Writers' Museum** (p41), which celebrates Edinburgh's literary heritage.

❹ St Giles Cathedral

Continue down the High St to **St Giles Cathedral** (p38), Edinburgh's most important church. Follow Parliament Sq around the south side of the church, and take a look at **Parliament Hall** (p40) and the **Mercat Cross** (p38).

❺ Real Mary King's Close

Back on the High St is the Georgian facade of the **city chambers** (seat of Edinburgh city council), which was built over a medieval Old Town alley with eerie remains you can explore on a tour of the **Real Mary King's Close** (p28).

❻ Museum of Edinburgh

Descend atmospheric **Advocate's Close**, then climb back to the Royal Mile along boutique-lined **Cockburn Street**. Continue down the High St, past **John Knox House** (p42), to the **Museum of Edinburgh** (p40), which records the city's history.

❼ Scottish Parliament Building

Opposite **Canongate Kirk**, go down Crighton's Close past the **Scottish Poetry Library** (p42), then left and left again up Reid's Close, to get a great view of the **Scottish Parliament Building** (p58).

❽ Palace of Holyroodhouse

The Royal Mile ends at the ornate gates of the **Palace of Holyroodhouse** (p56), the residence of the royal family when they're in town.

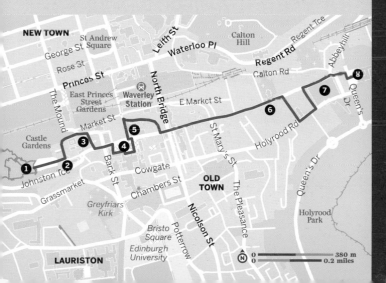

Best Walks
Charlotte Square to Calton Hill

🏃 The Walk

Edinburgh's New Town is one of the world's finest Georgian cityscapes, worthy of Unesco World Heritage status. This walk captures the essence of the New Town's Georgian elegance, taking in its two architecturally pivotal squares, the grand town houses of Heriot Row (complete with private gardens), and two of the city's best viewpoints, the Scott Monument and Calton Hill.

Start Charlotte Sq

Finish Calton Hill

Length 1.5 miles; one hour

✗ Take a Break

Thistle St, between Frederick and Hanover Sts, is home to a good selection of bistros and restaurants – try Café Marlayne (p81) for some French home cooking, or Fishers in the City (p83) for a seafood feast.

VISITBRITAIN/BRITAIN ON VIEW/GETTY IMAGES ©

Charlotte Square

❶ Charlotte Square

Charlotte Square (p76) is the jewel in the New Town's architectural crown, a masterpiece of neoclassical design. On the north side is the museum **Georgian House** (p76), while off the southeast corner is **16 South Charlotte Street**, birthplace of Alexander Graham Bell.

❷ Oxford Bar

Leave the square at its northeast corner and turn right along Young St, passing the **Oxford Bar** (p85), made famous by Ian Rankin's Inspector Rebus novels. Turn left on N Castle St, right on Queen St then left again, taking a peek into the private **Queen Street Gardens**.

❸ Heriot Row

Turn right into **Heriot Row**, a typically elegant New Town terrace. At No 17, an inscription marks the house where writer Robert Louis Stevenson spent his childhood. It's said that the island in the pond in Queen Street Gardens (not open to the public) was the inspiration for Treasure Island.

④ George Street

Go uphill to **George Street** and turn left. This was once the centre of Edinburgh's financial industry; now the banks and offices have been taken over by designer boutiques and cocktail bars. Pop into the **Dome Grill Room** at No 14, formerly a bank, to see the ornate Georgian banking hall.

⑤ St Andrew Square

The New Town's most impressive square is dominated by the

Melville Monument, commemorating Henry Dundas (1742–1811), the most powerful Scottish politician of his time. On the far side is **Dundas House**, a Palladian mansion that houses the head office of the Royal Bank of Scotland (another magnificent domed banking hall lies within)

⑥ Scott Monument

South St David St leads past **Jenners** (p72), the grand dame of Edinburgh department stores, to the **Scott**

Monument (p71). Climb the 287 steps to the top for an incomparable view over **Princes Street Gardens** (p70) to the castle.

⑦ Calton Hill

Head east along Princes St and Waterloo Pl to the stairs on the left just after the side street called Calton Hill. Climb to the summit of **Calton Hill** (p77), one of Edinburgh's finest viewpoints, with a panorama that stretches from the Firth of Forth to the Pentland Hills.

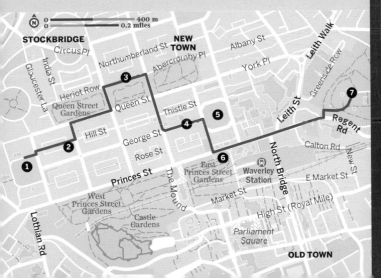

Best Eating

Eating out in Edinburgh has changed beyond all recognition in the last 20 years. Two decades ago, sophisticated dining meant a visit to the Aberdeen Angus Steak House for a prawn cocktail, steak (well done) and chips, and Black Forest gateau. Today, eating out has become a commonplace event and the city has more restaurants per head of population than any other city in the UK, including a handful of Michelin stars.

LONELY PLANET/GETTY IMAGES ©

Modern Scottish Cuisine

Scotland has never been celebrated for its national cuisine – in fact, from haggis and porridge to deep-fried Mars Bars, it has more often been an object of ridicule. But a new culinary style known as Modern Scottish has emerged, where chefs take top-quality Scottish produce – from Highland venison, Aberdeen Angus beef and freshly landed seafood to root vegetables, raspberries and Ayrshire cheeses – and prepare it simply, in a way that enhances the natural flavours, often adding a French, Italian or Asian twist.

Haggis – Scotland's National Dish

The raw ingredients of Scotland's national dish don't sound too promising – the finely chopped lungs, heart and liver of a sheep, mixed with oatmeal and onion and stuffed into a sheep's stomach bag. However, it actually tastes surprisingly good and is now on the menu in many of the capital's restaurants, whether served with the traditional accompaniment of *champit tatties* and *bashed neeps* (mashed potatoes and turnips), with a generous dollop of butter and a good sprinkling of black pepper, or given a modern twist (haggis in filo pastry parcels with hoisin sauce).

☑ **Top Tips**

▶ Book well in advance (at least a month ahead for August) to be sure of a table at Edinburgh's top restaurants.

▶ The *Edinburgh & Glasgow Eating & Drinking Guide* (www.list.co.uk/ead) contains reviews of around 800 restaurants, cafes and bars.

▶ The www.5pm. co.uk website lists last-minute offers from restaurants with tables to spare that evening.

Best Modern Scottish

Martin Wishart Edinburgh's first Michelin star still shines brightly, adding French flair to Scottish ingredients. (p116)

Timberyard Slow-food restaurant with emphasis on locally sourced produce. (p125)

Castle Terrace Seasonal menu makes the best of fine Scottish produce (p95)

Wedgwood Foraged salad leaves add originality to informal fine dining. (p134)

Plumed Horse Romantic atmosphere, elegant decor and great food. (p116)

The Kitchin Michelin-starred excellence from TV chef Tom Kitchin. (p116)

Best Traditional Scottish

Tower Specialities include Scottish oysters and Aberdeen Angus steaks, with a great view of the castle. (pictured left; p45)

Scottish Cafe & Restaurant Trad dishes such as Cullen skink and haggis served in National Gallery complex. (p71)

Amber Set in the Scotch Whisky Experience; many dishes include whisky in the recipe. (p45)

McKirdy's Steakhouse Prime Scottish beef, simply prepared and served in friendly informal setting. (p97)

Witchery by the Castle Wonderfully over-the-top Gothic decor, great steak and seafood, and fine wines. (p45)

Best Informal Dining

Gardener's Cottage Set menu of homegrown vegetables, foraged mushrooms and sustainable fish served at communal tables. (p81)

The Dogs Good-value bistro makes the most of cheaper cuts of meat; beef cheeks, oxtail, liver and onions. (p81)

Café Marlayne Cosy, famhouse kitchen atmosphere and tasty French home cooking. (p136)

Mums Retro cafe serving old-fashioned comfort food like sausages, mash and onion gravy. (p46)

Best Seafood

Ondine Arguably the best seafood restaurant in town, with low-lit romantic atmosphere. (p44)

Fishers Bistro Always busy and bustling, everything from humble fishcakes to the finest oysters. (p116)

Shore Pleasantly informal restaurant with Leith waterfront setting, serves game as well as seafood. (p117)

Best Vegetarian

David Bann Smart and sophisticated, brings an inventive approach to vegetarian food. (p45)

Kalpna Long-established Indian restaurant, famous for its all-you-can-eat lunch buffet. (p127)

Best **Drinking**

Edinburgh has always been a drinker's city. It has more than 700 pubs – more per square mile than any other UK city – and they are as varied and full of character as the people who drink in them, from Victorian palaces to stylish pre-club bars, and from real-ale howffs to trendy cocktail lounges.

Trad vs Trendy

At one end of Edinburgh's broad spectrum of hostelries lies the traditional 19th-century bar, which has preserved much of its original Victorian decoration and generally serves cask-conditioned real ales and a staggering range of malt whiskies. At the other end is the modern cocktail bar, with a cool clientele and styling so sharp you could cut yourself on it.

Edinburgh Beers

During the 19th century, Edinburgh ranked alongside Munich, Pilsen and Burton-on-Trent in importance as a brewing centre, and in the early 1900s laid claim to 28 breweries. Today, there are only two working breweries – Caledonian (now part-owned by Scottish and Newcastle) and Stewart's. Happily, this pair produce some of the finest beers in Britain, including Deuchar's IPA (available in most of the city's real-ale pubs) and Stewart's Edinburgh Gold.

Opening Times

Edinburgh pubs generally open from 11am to 11pm Monday to Saturday and 12.30pm to 11pm on Sunday. Many open later on Friday and Saturday, when they stay open till midnight or 1am, while those with a food or music licence can party on until 3am. The bell for last orders rings about 15 minutes before closing time, and you're allowed 15 minutes' drinking-up time after the bar closes.

☑ **Top Tips**

▶ The Gig Guide (www.gigguide.co.uk) is a free monthly email newsletter and listings website covering live music in Edinburgh pubs.

▶ If you want to avoid the crowds on Friday and Saturday nights, steer clear of the Grassmarket, the Cowgate and Lothian Rd.

Best Historic Pubs

Bennet's Bar Locals' pub with lovely Victorian fittings, from stained glass to brass water taps on bar. (pictured above right; p127)

Café Royal Circle Bar City-centre haven of

Bennet's Bar (p127)

Victorian splendour, famed for Doulton ceramic portraits. (p84)

Sheep Heid Inn Semi-rural retreat in the shadow of Arthur's Seat, famed as Edinburgh's oldest pub. (p61)

Guildford Arms A time-capsule of polished mahogany and gleaming brass. (p84)

Best Real-Ale Bars

Holyrood 9A Modern take on trad pub, with no fewer than 20 beers on tap. (p47)

Blue Blazer Resolutely old-fashioned pub with good range of Scottish ales. (p127)

Stockbridge Tap More lounge bar than pub, but with seven real ales on offer. (p108)

BrewDog Lively modern bar owned by one of Scotland's most innovative microbreweries. (pictured left; p46)

Auld Hoose Great jukebox plus broad range of beers from Scottish microbreweries. (p128)

Best Cocktail Bars

Bramble Possibly the city's best cocktails, served in an atmospheric cellar bar. (p84)

Amicus Apple Informal lounge that creates its own unusual mixes as well as expertly prepared classics. (p85)

Tigerlily Cocktails as colourful as the swirling, glittering designer decor. (p86)

Villager Laid-back, sofa-strewn lounge serving great cocktails without the faff. (p48)

Best Whisky Bars

Bow Bar Busy Grassmarket-area pub with huge selection of malt whiskies (plus good range of boutique gins) (p46)

Malt Shovel Old-school pub with more than 100 single malts behind the bar. (p48)

Cumberland Bar Good summer choice; enjoy your malt while sitting in the garden. (p85)

Best
Shopping

Edinburgh's shopping experience extends far beyond the big-name department stores of Princes St, ranging from designer fashion and handmade jewellery to independent bookshops, delicatessens and farmers markets. Classic north-of-the-border buys include cashmere, Harris tweed, tartan goods, Celtic jewellery, smoked salmon and Scotch whisky.

VISITBRITAIN/CHRIS COE/GETTY IMAGES ©

Princes Street

Princes St is Edinburgh's trademark shopping strip, lined with all the big high-street stores from Marks & Spencer to BHS and Debenhams, with more upmarket designer shops a block north on George St, and many smaller specialist stores on Rose St and Thistle St. There are also two big city-centre shopping malls – **Princes Mall**, at the eastern end of Princes St next to the Balmoral Hotel, and the nearby **St James Centre**, at the top of Leith St – plus **Multrees Walk**, a designer shopping complex with a flagship Harvey Nichols store on the eastern side of St Andrew Sq.

Shopping Districts

Other central shopping streets include South Bridge, Nicolson St and Lothian Rd. For more offbeat shopping – including fashion, music, crafts, gifts and jewellery – head for the cobbled lanes of Cockburn, Victoria and St Mary's Sts, all leading off the Royal Mile in the Old Town; William St in the West End; and Raeburn Pl and St Stephen's St in Stockbridge. Ocean Terminal, in Leith, is the city's biggest shopping mall.

☑ Top Tips

▶ In shops displaying a 'Tax Free' sign, visitors from non-EU countries can claim back the 20% VAT (value-added tax) they have paid on purchased goods.

▶ Many city-centre shops stay open till 7pm or 8pm on Thursdays.

Best Department Stores

Jenners The mother of all Edinburgh department stores, founded in 1838. (pictured above right; p72)

Harvey Nichols Four floors of designer labels, plus rooftop brasserie with grand views. (p73)

Jenners (p72)

Best for Tartan

Kinloch Anderson
Tailors and kiltmakers to
HM the Queen and HRH
the Duke of Edinburgh;
'nuff said. (p119)

Geoffrey (Tailor) Inc
Kilts in all colours from
clan tartans to camou-
flage to black leather.
(p53)

Best for Jewellery

Galerie Mirages An
Aladdin's cave of jewel-
lery and gifts in both
ethnic and contemporary
designs. (p109)

Alchemia Original de-
signs as well as specially
commissioned pieces.
(p73)

Annie Smith Edinburgh
designer famed for
beautiful and delicate
pieces reflecting nature's
patterns. (p108)

Best for Books

Word Power Long-
established radical
bookshop specialising in
political, gay and feminist
literature. (p129)

**McNaughtan's Book-
shop** Secondhand and
antiquarian dealer, books
on Scottish history, art
and architecture. (p88)

Best Markets

**Edinburgh Farmers
Market** Saturday feast of
fresh Scottish produce,
from smoked venison to
organic free-range eggs.
(p96)

Stockbridge Market
Eclectic Sunday market
that has become a focus
for the local community.
(p105)

Best **Views**

Edinburgh is one of Europe's most beautiful cities, draped across a series of rocky hills overlooking the sea. A glance in any souvenir shop will reveal a display of postcards that testify to the city's many viewpoints, both natural and artificial. Part of the pleasure of any visit to Edinburgh is simply soaking up the scenery, so set aside some time to explore the loftier parts of the city, camera in hand.

LONELY PLANET/GETTY IMAGES ©

Best Natural Viewpoints

Arthur's Seat Sweeping panoramas from the highest point in Edinburgh. (p63)

Calton Hill Edinburgh's templed 'acropolis' affords a superb view along Princes St. (p77)

Blackford Hill This southern summit provides a grandstand view of Castle Rock and Arthur's Seat. (p124)

Best Architectural Viewpoints

Scott Monument Climb 287 steps to the top of this Gothic pinnacle and look out over Princes Street Gardens. (p71)

Camera Obscura The outlook tower here provides an iconic view along the Royal Mile. (p43)

Castle Esplanade Commanding views north across the New Town, or south towards the Pentland Hills. (p24)

Best Restaurant Views

Tower Perched at the top of the National Museum of Scotland, with a superb view of the castle. (p45)

Maxie's Bistro Outdoor tables on Victoria Terrace look out over Victoria St to the Grassmarket. (p34)

Scottish Cafe & Restaurant The window tables here have a lovely outlook along Princes Street Gardens. (p71)

Best
For Kids

Edinburgh has a multitude of attractions for children, and most things to see and do are child-friendly. During the Edinburgh and Fringe Festivals there's lots of street theatre for kids, especially on High St and at the foot of the Mound, and in December there's a Ferris wheel, an open-air ice rink and fairground rides in Princes Street Gardens.

VISITBRITAIN/BR TPIN ON VIEW/GETTY IMAGES ©

Best Sights for Kids

Edinburgh Castle Ask about the Children's Trail at the ticket office, which lets kids track down various treasures. (p24)

Edinburgh Zoo Giant pandas, interactive chimpanzee enclosure, penguins on parade... (p85)

Our Dynamic Earth Loads of great stuff, from earthquake simulators to real icebergs. (pictured above right; p63)

Camera Obscura Fascinating exhibits on illusions, magic tricks, electricity and holograms. (p43)

Real Mary King's Close Older children enjoy the ghost stories and creepy atmosphere here. (p28)

Scott Monument Lots of narrow stairs to climb, grotesque carvings to spot, and a view at the top. (p71)

Best Museums for Kids

National Museum of Scotland Lots of interactive exhibits, and trail leaflots for kids to follow and fill in. (p30)

Scottish National Gallery of Modern Art Great landscaped ground for exploring – track down all the sculptures! (p92)

City Art Centre Runs a series of events for kids, from art workshops to learning magic tricks. (p43)

☑ Top Tips

▶ The Edinburgh Information Centre (p160) has lots of info on children's events, and you can find the handy guidebook *Edinburgh for Under Fives* in most bookshops.

▶ Kids under five travel for free on Edinburgh buses, and five- to 15-year-olds pay a flat fare of 70p.

Best
Museums &
Galleries

As Scotland's capital city, it's hardly surprising that Edinburgh is home to some of the country's most important museums and art collections. You can admire the old masters, from Titian to Turner, at the Scottish National Gallery, hone your knowledge of Scottish heritage at the National Museum of Scotland, or delve into the arcane delights of the city's less-well-known museums.

KARL BLACKWELL/GETTY IMAGES © ARTWORK: SAINT SEBASTIAN BOUND FOR MARTYRDOM, ARTIST: SIR ANTHONY VAN DYCK

☑ Top Tips

▶ The national collections have useful 'trail' leaflets that guide you around their highlights.

▶ All major museums and galleries have good restaurants or cafes, often worth a visit in their own right.

Museums & Galleries by Night

Several of the city's major institutions host 'after hours' events. The National Galleries hold several 'Gallery by Night' events each year, with music, drama and comedy performances linked to current exhibitions, while the National Museum of Scotland stages Saturday-night 'Museum After Hours' events during the Festival Fringe, with live music, performers, drinks and snacks. Check websites for details.

Admission & Access

National collections (eg National Museum of Scotland, Scottish National Gallery, Scottish National Portrait Gallery, Scottish National Gallery of Modern Art) and Edinburgh city-owned museums (Museum of Edinburgh, City Art Centre etc) have free admission, except for temporary exhibitions where a fee is often charged. Most private galleries are also free, while smaller museums often charge an entrance fee, typically around £5 (book online at some museums for discounted tickets). National collections are generally open from 10am to 5pm, with the Scottish National Gallery and Scottish National Portrait Gallery staying open till 7pm on Thursdays.

Best Collections

National Museum of Scotland Beautiful setting for collections covering Scottish history, the natural world, art and engineering. (p30)

Scottish National Portrait Gallery Far more interesting than the name implies, especially after a recent revamp. (p68)

Scottish National Portrait Gallery (p68)

Scottish National Gallery Old masters (pictured left), Scottish artists, and Canova's famous marble sculpture of the *Three Graces*. (p76)

Scottish National Gallery of Modern Art Pride of place goes to works by the Scottish Colourists, Eduardo Paolozzi and Barbara Hepworth. (p92)

Best Smaller Museums

Museum of Edinburgh The city; Stone Age to 20th century. (p40)

People's Story The life and work of ordinary Edinburgh folk from the 18th century onward. (p43)

Surgeons' Hall Museums Grisly but fascinating collection on the history of surgery. (p124)

Writers' Museum All you ever wanted to know about Robert Burns, Walter Scott and Robert Louis Stevenson. (p41)

Best Museum Architecture

Scottish National Portrait Gallery Gorgeous palace in Venetian Gothic style, studded with sculptures of famous Scots. (pictured above; p68)

National Museum of Scotland Staid Victorian building set off by flamboyant modern extension in golden sandstone. (p30)

Museum of Edinburgh Set in a 16th-century house with colourful and ornate decoration in red and yellow ochre. (p40)

Worth a Trip

The grounds of 19th-century Bonnington House, 10 miles west of Edinburgh, have been converted into a gorgeous sculpture park called **Jupiter Artland** (📞 01506-889 900; www.jupiterartland. org; Bonnington House Steadings, Wilkieston; adult/child £8.50/4.50; ⏰ 10am-5pm Thu-Sun late May–mid-Sep). It showcases works by a clutch of Britain's leading artists. First Edinburgh bus 27 departs every 30 minutes (hourly on Sunday) from stops on Princes St and Dalry Rd.

Best **Festivals & Events**

Edinburgh is one of the biggest party venues in the world, with a crowded calendar of contrasting festivals ranging from science and storytelling to music, movies and military bands. High season is August, when half a dozen festivals – including the huge Edinburgh International Festival, and the even bigger Festival Fringe – run concurrently. It's closely followed by December, when the Christmas festival runs into the Hogmanay celebrations.

Edinburgh International Festival

First held in 1947 to mark a return to peace after the ordeal of WWII, the Edinburgh International Festival is festooned with superlatives – the oldest, the biggest, the most famous, the best in the world. The festival takes place over the three weeks ending on the first Saturday in September; the program is usually available from April. Tickets sell out quickly, so it's best to book as far in advance as possible.

Edinburgh Festival Fringe

When the first Edinburgh International Festival was held in 1947, there were eight theatre companies that didn't make it onto the main program. Undeterred, they grouped together and held their own mini-festival, on the fringe, and an Edinburgh institution was born. The Fringe takes place over 3½ weeks, the last two overlapping with the first two of the Edinburgh International Festival.

Big-name tickets can cost £15 and up, but there are plenty of good shows in the £5 to £10 range and lots of free stuff. Fringe Sunday – usually the second Sunday – is a smorgasbord of free performances, staged in the Meadows park to the south of the city centre.

VISITBRITAIN/PAWEL LIBERA/GETTY IMAGES ©

☑ Top Tips

▶ *The List* (£2.50; www.list.co.uk) is a fortnightly events and listings magazine (also covering Glasgow), available from most newsagents. It has competition in the form of *The Skinny* (www.theskinny. co.uk), another listings mag covering both Edinburgh and Glasgow.

Best Festivals

Edinburgh International Science Festival

Hosts a wide range of events, including talks, lectures, exhibitions, demonstrations, guided tours and interactive experiments designed to stimulate, inspire and challenge; April.

Christmas in Edinburgh

Imaginate Festival
Britain's biggest festival of performing arts for children, with events suitable for kids aged three to 12. Groups from around the world perform classic tales like *Hansel and Gretel*, as well as new material written specially for children; May.

Edinburgh International Film Festival
The two-week film festival is a major international event, serving as a showcase for new British and European films, and staging the European premieres of one or two Hollywood blockbusters; June.

Edinburgh International Festival
Hundreds of the world's top musicians and performers congregate for three weeks of diverse and inspirational music, opera, theatre and dance, August.

Edinburgh Festival Fringe
The biggest festival of the performing arts anywhere in the world; August.

Edinburgh Military Tattoo
A spectacular display of military marching bands (pictured left), massed pipes and drums, acrobats, cheerleaders and motorcycle display teams, all played out in front of the magnificent backdrop of the floodlit castle; August.

Edinburgh International Book Festival
A fun fortnight of talks, readings, debates, lectures, book signings and meet-the-author events, with a cafe and tented bookshop thrown in; August.

Best Events

Beltane
A pagan fire festival, resurrected in modern form, marking the end of winter, celebrated on the summit of Calton Hill. Held on the night of 30 April into the early hours of 1 May.

Royal Highland Show
A four-day feast of all things rural, from tractor driving to sheep shearing; late June.

Edinburgh's Christmas
Includes a street parade, fairground and Ferris wheel, and an open-air ice rink in Princes Street Gardens (pictured above); December.

Edinburgh's Hogmanay
Events run from 29 December to 1 January, and include a torchlight procession and huge street party.

Best
Architecture

Edinburgh's unique beauty arises from a combination of its unusual site, perched among craggy hills, and a legacy of fine architecture dating from the 16th century to the present day. The New Town remains the world's most complete and unspoilt example of Georgian architecture and town planning. Along with the Old Town, it was declared a Unesco World Heritage Site in 1995.

Old Town Tenements

One of the features of the Old Town is the biggest concentration of surviving 17th-century buildings in Britain. These tenements, six to eight storeys high, were among the tallest in Britain in their time. You can explore such tenements at Gladstone's Land (p41) and John Knox House (pictured right; p42).

Georgian Gorgeousness

Robert Adam (1728–92), one of the leading architects of the Georgian period, made his mark in Edinburgh's New Town with neoclassical masterpieces such as Charlotte Sq (p76) and Edinburgh University's Old College. Experience the elegance of Adam's interiors by visiting the Georgian House (p76).

Modern Masterpiece

The plan for the New Town was the result of a competition won by James Craig, then an unknown, self-taught 23-year-old. At the end of the 20th century another architectural competition resulted in the relatively unknown Enric Miralles being chosen as the architect for the new Scottish Parliament Building (p58). Though its construction was shrouded with controversy, the building won the 2005 Stirling Prize for the best new architecture in Britain, and has revitalised a near-derelict industrial site at the foot of the Royal Mile.

DE AGOSTINI/W BUSS/GETTY IMAGES ©

☑ Top Tip

▶ The website www.edinburgh architecture.co.uk is crammed with useful info, including guided architectural walking tours.

Best Modern Architecture

Scottish Parliament Building Ambitious, controversial and way over budget; the most exciting example of modern architecture in Scotland. (p58)

National Museum of Scotland The museum's golden sandstone lines create echoes of castles, churches, gardens and cliffs. (p30)

Scottish Poetry Library Award-winning building, cleverly insinuated into a cramped space in an Old Town alley. (p42)

Front Range The designer glasshouses in Edinburgh's Royal Botanic Garden, built in 1967, are included in *Prospect* magazine's Top 100 Modern Scottish Buildings. (p102)

Best Neoclassical Architecture

Charlotte Square The elegantly proportioned Adam facade on the square's north side is the jewel in the New Town's architectural crown (p76)

Royal Scottish Academy Recently stone-cleaned, this imposing William Playfair–designed Doric temple dominates the centre of Princes St. (p76)

Dundas House Gorgeous Palladian mansion that now houses a bank; pop into the main hall for a look at the dome, painted blue and studded with glazed stars. (p137)

Best Early Architecture

George Heriot's School Imposing renaissance building (1628–1650), funded by George Heriot (nicknamed Jinglin' Geordie), goldsmith and jeweller to King James VI. (p35)

Parliament Hall Dating from 1639, this grandiose hall has a majestic hammer-beam roof, and was home to the Scottish Parliament until the 1707 Act of Union. (p40)

Best Monuments

Scott Monument This Gothic space rocket parked amid the greenery of Princes Street Gardens celebrates Scotland's most famous historical novelist, Sir Walter Scott. (p71)

Nelson Monument Built in the shape of an upturned telescope, this slender tower on the summit of Calton Hill was built to commemorate Nelson's victory at Trafalgar in 1805. (p77)

Melville Monument Edinburgh's answer to London's Nelson's Column towers over St Andrew Sq, topped by a statue of Henry Dundas (1742–1811), the most powerful Scottish politician of his time. (p137)

National Monument An unfinished folly atop Calton Hill; its Greek temple–like appearance gave Edinburgh the nickname 'Athens of the North' (p78)

Best Tours

Best Walking Tours

City of the Dead Tours
(www.cityofthedeadtours.
com; adult/concession
£10/8) This tour of
Greyfriars Kirkyard is
probably the scariest
of Edinburgh's 'ghost'
tours. Many people have
reported encounters with
the 'McKenzie Poltergeist', the ghost of a
17th-century judge
who persecuted the
Covenanters, and now
haunts their former
prison in a corner of the
kirkyard. Not suitable for
young children.

Edinburgh Literary Pub
Tour (www.edinburghliterary
pubtour.co.uk; adult/student
£14/10) An enlightening
two-hour trawl through
Edinburgh's literary
history – and its associated howffs (meeting
places, often pubs) – in
the entertaining company of Messrs Clart and
McBrain. One of the city's
best walking tours.

Mercat Tours (www.
mercattours.com; adult/child
£10/5) Mercat offers a
wide range of fascinating
history walks and 'Ghosts
& Ghouls' tours, but its
most famous is a visit
to the hidden, haunted,
underground vaults
beneath South Bridge.

Cadies & Witchery
Tours (www.witcherytours.
com; adult/child £8.50/6)
The becloaked and
pasty-faced Adam Lyal
(deceased) leads a
'Murder & Mystery' tour
of the Old Town's darker
corners. These tours are
famous for their 'jumperooters' – costumed
actors who 'jump oot'
when you least expect it.

Rebus Tours (www.rebus
tours.com; adult/student
£10/9) A two-hour guided
tour of the 'hidden Edinburgh' frequented by novelist Ian Rankin's fictional
detective, John Rebus.
Not recommended for
children under 10.

Best Bus Tours

Majestic Tour (www.
edinburghtour.com; adult/
child £13/6) Hop-on/hop-off tour departing every
15 to 20 minutes from
Waverley Bridge to the
Royal Yacht Britannia at
Ocean Terminal via the
New Town, Royal Botanic
Garden and Newhaven,
returning via Leith Walk,
Holyrood and the Royal
Mile.

MacTours (www.edinburgh
tour.com; adult/child £13/6)
A quick tour around the
highlights of the Old
and New Towns, from
the castle to Calton Hill,
aboard an open-topped
vintage bus.

Survival Guide

Survival Guide

Before You Go

When to Go

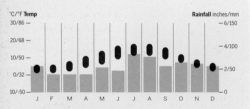

→ Winter (Dec–Feb)
Cold and dark, occasional snow; Christmas decorations, Hogmanay and Burns Night celebrations.

→ Spring (Mar–May)
Cold to mild, damp, occasional sun; flowers and blossom everywhere.

→ Summer (Jun–Aug)
Mild to warm but occasionally wet; main tourist season, city packed out for festival in August.

→ Autumn (Sep–Nov)
Mild to chilly, often damp; autumn colours in parks, tourist crowds have left.

Book Your Stay

→ Hotels and hostels are found throughout the Old and New Towns; midrange B&Bs and guesthouses are concentrated outside the centre in the suburbs of Tollcross, Bruntsfield, Newington and Pilrig.

→ If you're driving, don't even think about staying in the city centre unless your hotel has its own private car park – parking in the centre is a nightmare.

→ Edinburgh is packed to the gills during the festival period (August) and over Hogmanay (New Year). If you want a room during these periods, book as far in advance as you can – a year ahead if possible.

→ It's best to book at least a few months ahead for accommodation at Easter and from mid-May to mid-September.

→ Edinburgh accommodation costs: budget is less than £60, midrange £60 to £150, and top end is more than £150, based on the cost of a double room with breakfast.

➡ If you're staying for a week or more, a short-term or serviced apartment might be more economical.

➡ Edinburgh Information Centre (p160) has a last-minute booking service; £5 fee.

Useful Websites

Lonely Planet (www.lonelyplanet.com/hotels) Bookings.

Edinburgh & the Lothians (www.edinburgh.org) Official tourist website, with wide range of accommodation and weekend break offers.

Best Budget

Edinburgh Central SYHA (☎524 2090; www.edinburghcentral.org; 9 Haddington Pl, Leith Walk; dm/s/tw £25/49/74; @ 📶) Hostelling Scotland's five-star establishment close to the city centre.

Smart City Hostel (☎0870 892 3000; www.smartcityhostels.com; 50 Blackfriars St; dm from £22, tr £107; @ 📶) A big (620 beds), bright, modern

hostel in the heart of the Old Town.

Argyle Backpackers (☎667 9991; www.argyle-backpackers.co.uk; 14 Argyle Pl; dm £17-22, d & tw £45-65; 📶) A quiet and relaxed hostel in terraced house with conservatory and walled garden.

Malone's Old Town Hostel (☎226 7040; www.maloneshostel.com; 14 Forrest Rd; dm £20-25; @ 📶) Comfortable new hostel above an Irish pub, just south of Royal Mile.

Best Midrange

Sheridan Guest House (☎554 4107; www.sheridanedinburgh.co.uk; 1 Bonnington Tce, Newhaven Rd; s/d from £55/70; 📶) A little haven hidden away to the north of the New Town.

Southside Guest House (☎668 4422; www.southsideguesthouse.co.uk; 8 Newington Rd; s/d £70/90; 📶) South Edinburgh town house, feels more like a modern boutique hotel.

Millers 64 (☎454 3666; www.millers64.com; 64 Pilrig St; s from £80, d £90-150; 📶) Luxury Victorian town house halfway between New Town and Leith.

Ardmor House (☎554 4944; www.ardmorhouse.com; 74 Pilrig St; s £60-85, d £85-170; 📶) Gay-owned and straight-friendly; a stylishly renovated town house just off Leith Walk.

Best Top End

Hotel Missoni (☎220 6666; www.hotelmissoni.com; 1 George IV Bridge; r £90-225; 📶) Italian style icon in the heart of the medieval Old Town.

Witchery by the Castle (☎225 5613; www.thewitchery.com; Castlehill, Royal Mile; ste £325-350) Eight lavish Gothic suites in the shadow of Edinburgh Castle.

Tigerlily (☎225 5005; www.tigerlilyedinburgh.co.uk; 125 George St; r from £175; 📶) Georgian meets gorgeous at this glamorous New Town boutique hotel.

Knight Residence (☎622 8120; www.theknightresidence.co.uk; 12 Lauriston St; d/2-bedroom apt £250/437; 📶) Luxury serviced apartments in a quiet street only a few minutes' walk from the Grassmarket.

Arriving in Edinburgh

☑ **Top Tip** For the best way to get to your accommodation, see p17.

Edinburgh Airport

About 8 miles west of the city centre, **Edinburgh Airport** (EDI; www.edinburghairport.com) has numerous flights to other parts of Scotland and the UK, Ireland and mainland Europe.

➡ **Lothian Buses Airlink** (www.flybybus.com) Bus service 100 runs from the airport to Waverley Bridge, outside the main train station, via Haymarket and the West End every 10 minutes from 4am to midnight, every 30 minutes through the night (£3.50/6 one way/return, 30 minutes).

➡ **Taxi** An airport taxi to the city centre costs around £16 to £18 and takes about 20 minutes. Taxis depart from outside the arrivals hall; go out through the main doors and turn left.

➡ **Tram** (www.edinburgh trams.com) Service scheduled to begin in summer 2014. Trams run from the airport to York Pl in the city centre via Princes St.

Edinburgh Waverley Train Station

The main train station is Edinburgh Waverley, located in the heart of the city between the Old Town and New Town. Trains arriving from, and departing for, the west also stop at Edinburgh Haymarket station, which is more convenient for the West End.

Getting Around

Bus

☑ **Best for...** getting around the city.

➡ The main bus operators are **Lothian Buses** (www.lothianbuses.com) and **First** (☏ 663 9233; www.first edinburgh.co.uk); for timetable information contact **Traveline** (☏ 0871 200 22 33; www.travelinescotland.com).

➡ Bus timetables, route maps and fare guides are posted at all main bus stops.

➡ You can pick up a copy of the free *Lothian Buses Route Map* from Lothian Buses Travelshops.

➡ Adult fares are £1.50 per single journey; purchase from the driver. Children aged under five travel free and those aged five to 15 pay a flat fare of 70p.

➡ Night-service buses (www.nightbuses.com) run hourly between midnight and 5am, flat fare £3 for all-night travel.

Tram

☑ **Best for...** getting to and from the airport.

➡ Edinburgh's new **tram system** (www.edinburgh trams.com) is scheduled to begin service in summer 2014.

➡ The line runs from Edinburgh Airport to York Pl, at the top of Leith Walk, via Haymarket, the West End and Princes St.

➡ Tickets are integrated with the city's Lothian Buses, costing £1.50 for a single journey.

➡ Trams should run every 12 minutes from the airport, every six minutes in the city centre.

Taxi
☑ **Best for...** late-night journeys.

➡ Edinburgh's black taxis can be hailed in the street, ordered by phone, or picked up at one of the many central ranks:

Central Taxis (☏ 229 2468)

City Cabs (☏ 228 1211)

ComCab (☏ 272 8000)

➡ The minimum charge is £2 (£3 at night) for the first 450m, then 25p for every subsequent 195m or 42 seconds – a typical 2-mile trip across the city centre will cost around £6 to £7.

➡ Tipping is up to you – because of the high fares local people rarely tip on short journeys, but occasionally round up to the nearest 50p on longer ones.

Bicycle
☑ **Best for...** short distances, and escaping to the countryside. Beware of city-centre hills!

➡ Edinburgh is well equipped with bike lanes and dedicated cycle tracks.

➡ You can buy a map of the city's cycle routes from most bike shops.

➡ **Biketrax** (☏ 228 6633; www.biketrax.co.uk; 11-13 Lochrin Pl; ⏰ 9.30am-6pm Mon-Fri to 5.30pm Sat, noon-5pm Sun; 🚌 all Tollcross buses) rents out a wide range of cycles and equipment, including kids' bikes, tandems, recumbents, pannier bags and child seats. A mountain bike costs £16 for 24 hours.

Car & Motorcycle
☑ **Best for...** independence.

➡ Though useful for day trips beyond the city, a car in central Edinburgh is more of a liability than a convenience; finding a parking place in the city centre is like striking gold.

➡ All the big, international car-rental agencies have offices in Edinburgh:

Avis (☏ 0844 544 6059; www.avis.co.uk; 24 East London St)

Budget (☏ 455 7314; www.budget.co.uk; Waverley Train Station, Waverley Bridge)

Europcar (☏ 0871 384 3453; www.europcar.co.uk; Waverley Train Station, Waverley Bridge)

Tickets & Passes

➡ **Daysaver ticket** (£3.50; available from drivers of Lothian Buses) gives unlimited travel (on Lothian Buses only, excluding night buses) for a day.

➡ **Ridacard** (£17; available from Travelshops, but not from bus drivers) gives unlimited bus travel on Lothian Buses for one week.

➡ There are many smaller, local agencies that offer better rates, including **Arnold Clark** (☏ 657 9120; www.arnoldclarkrental.co.uk; 20 Seafield Rd East).

Essential Information

Business Hours
Listings in this book won't include opening hours unless they differ significantly from these standard hours:

Banks 9.30am-4pm Mon-Fri, some branches 9.30am-1pm Sat

Businesses 9am-5pm Mon-Fri

Pubs and bars 11am-11pm Mon-Thu, 11am-1am Fri & Sat, 12.30pm-11pm Sun

Restaurants noon-2.30pm & 6-10pm

Shops 9am-5.30pm Mon-Sat, some to 8pm Thu, 11am-5pm Sun

Discount Cards

➡ **Royal Edinburgh Ticket** (www.edinburghtour.com; adult/child £45/25) Gives two days' unlimited travel on sightseeing buses, plus admission to Edinburgh Castle, Palace of Holyroodhouse and Royal Yacht Britannia.

➡ **Edinburgh Pass** (www.edinburgh.org/pass; 1/2/3 days £30/40/50) Offers free entry to more than 30 attractions and tours, plus unlimited travel on Lothian Buses services and one return journey on the Airlink 100 airport bus. As yet, entry to Edinburgh Castle and the Royal Yacht Britannia are not included in the pass.

Electricity

230V/50Hz

Emergency

In in emergency, dial ☎999 or ☎112 to call the police, ambulance, fire brigade or coastguard.

Money

Currency

➡ The unit of currency in the UK is the pound sterling (£).

➡ One pound sterling consists of 100 pence (called 'p' colloquially).

➡ Banknotes come in denominations of £5, £10, £20 and £50.

➡ Scottish banks issue their own banknotes, meaning there's quite a variety of different notes in circulation. They are harder to exchange outside the UK, so swap for Bank of England notes before you leave.

ATMs

➡ Automatic teller machines (ATMs – often called cashpoints) are widespread.

➡ You can use Visa, MasterCard, Amex, Cirrus, Plus and Maestro to withdraw cash from ATMs belonging to most banks and building societies.

➡ Cash withdrawals from non-bank ATMs, usually found in shops, may be subject to a charge of £1.50 or £2.

Credit Cards

➡ Visa and MasterCard are widely accepted, though some small businesses will charge for accepting them.

➡ Charge cards such as Amex and Diners Club are less widely used.

Money Changers

➡ The best-value place to change money is at post offices, where no commission is charged.

Money-Saving Tips

➡ Many Edinburgh restaurants, including the Michelin-starred ones, offer good lunch deals. Look out also for 'early bird' specials (usually available between 5pm and 7pm).

➡ All national museums and galleries are free, as are all Edinburgh city-council-owned museums.

➡ Be careful using bureaux de change; they may offer good exchange rates but frequently levy outrageous commissions and fees.

Tipping

➡ Tip 10% in sit-down restaurants, but not if they've already added a service charge to the bill. In classy places they may expect closer to 15%.

Public Holidays

New Year's Day
1 January

New Year Bank Holiday
2 January

Spring Bank Holiday
second Monday in April

Good Friday Friday before Easter Sunday

Easter Monday Monday following Easter Sunday

May Day Holiday first Monday in May

Christmas Day
25 December

Boxing Day
26 December

➡ Edinburgh also has its own local holidays on the third Monday in May and the third Monday in September, when post offices and some shops and businesses are closed.

Safe Travel

➡ Keep your passport, cash and credit cards separate.

➡ Edinburgh is a relatively safe city, so exercising common sense should keep you safe.

➡ Women should avoid crossing the Meadows (the park that lies between the Old Town and Marchmont) alone after dark.

Telephone

➡ There are plenty of public phones in Edinburgh, operated by either coins, phonecards or credit cards; phonecards are available in newsagents.

➡ Edinburgh's area code is 0131, followed by a seven-digit number. You only need to dial the 0131 prefix when you are calling Edinburgh from outside the city, or if you're dialling from a mobile.

Mobile Phones

➡ The UK uses the GSM 900/1800 network, which is compatible with the rest of Europe, Australia and New Zealand, but not with the North American GSM 1900 system or Japanese mobile technology.

➡ If in doubt, check with your service provider; some North Americans have GSM 1900/900 phones that will work in the UK.

➡ Edinburgh has excellent 3G coverage.

Phone Codes

International dialling code 📞 00

Edinburgh area code 📞 0131

Mobile phone numbers
📞07

Local call rate 📞0845;
from UK landlines; 15p
to 40p per minute from
mobiles

National call rate
📞0870; from UK
landlines; 15p to 40p per
minute from mobiles

Premium call rate 📞09;
£1.50 per minute

Toll-free numbers
📞0800 or 0808; from
UK landlines; 15p to 30p
per minute from mobiles

**Making International
Calls**

➔ To call abroad from
the UK, dial the inter-
national access code
(📞00), then the area
code (dropping any
initial 0) followed by the
telephone number.

Useful Numbers

**International directory
enquiries** 📞153

International operator
📞155

**Local & national
directory enquiries**
📞118 500

**Local & national
operator** 📞100

**Reverse-charge/collect
calls** 📞155

Speaking clock 📞123

Toilets

➔ Public toilets, free to
use, are spread across
the city; most are open
10am to 8pm. Find the
nearest one at www.
edinburgh.gov.uk; search
for 'public toilet'.

Tourist Information

**Edinburgh Informa-
tion Centre** (Map p36, D1;
📞473 3868; www.edinburgh.
org; Princes Mall, 3 Princes
St; ⏰9am-9pm Mon-Sat,
10am-8pm Sun Jul & Aug,
9am-7pm Mon-Sat, 10am-
7pm Sun May-Jun & Sep,
9am-5pm Mon-Wed, to 6pm
Thu-Sun Oct-Apr) Includes
an accommodation
booking service, currency
exchange, gift- and book-
shop, internet access and
counters selling tickets
for Edinburgh city tours
and Scottish Citylink bus
services.

**Edinburgh Airport
Information Centre**
(📞344 3120; main con-
course, Edinburgh Airport;
⏰7.30am-9pm)

**Travellers with
Disabilities**

➔ Edinburgh's Old Town,
with its steep hills, narrow
closes, flights of stairs
and cobbled streets, is a

Dos & Don'ts

Do

➔ Buy your round in the pub; Scots take it in
turns to buy a round of drinks for the whole
group.

➔ Shake hands on first meeting.

➔ Form an orderly queue!

Don't

➔ Drop litter or cigarette ends on Edinburgh's
streets; you can be nailed with an on-the-spot
fine.

➔ Forget your umbrella or waterproof jacket.

➔ Smoke on public transport or in pubs,
restaurants and other enclosed public places.

challenge for wheelchair users.

➡ Large new hotels and modern tourist attractions are usually fine; however, many B&Bs and guesthouses are in hard-to-adapt older buildings that lack ramps and lifts.

➡ Newer buses have steps or suspension that lowers for access, but it's wise to check before setting out. Most black taxis are wheelchair-friendly.

➡ Many banks are fitted with induction loops to assist the hearing impaired. Some attractions have Braille guides for the visually impaired.

➡ **VisitScotland** (www.visitscotland.com) has an online guide to accessible accommodation for travellers with disabilities.

Visas

➡ Visa regulations are subject to change so it's essential to check before travelling – see www.ukvisas.gov.uk or your local British embassy.

➡ Visas are not required for visitors from the European Economic Area.

➡ Those from Australia, Canada, New Zealand, South Africa and the USA need visas for study and work, but only for tourism if they stay more than six months.

➡ Other nationalities require visas.

Behind the Scenes

Send Us Your Feedback

We love to hear from travellers – your comments help make our books better. We read every word, and we guarantee that your feedback goes straight to the authors. Visit **lonelyplanet.com/contact** to submit your updates and suggestions.

Note: We may edit, reproduce and incorporate your comments in Lonely Planet products such as guidebooks, websites and digital products, so let us know if you don't want your comments reproduced or your name acknowledged. For a copy of our privacy policy visit lonelyplanet.com/privacy.

Our Readers

Many thanks to the travellers who used the last edition and wrote to us with helpful hints, useful advice and interesting anecdotes:

Claes Jansson, Mark Vero.

Neil's Thanks

Many thanks to Carol Downie, Steve Hall, Squid, Guzzle, Keith, Steven, Tom, Christine, Brendan and all the other reprobates who provided moral and financial (and occasionally physical) support during the arduous task of researching pubs and restaurants. Thanks also to the travellers who chipped in with recommendations, and to the various people I pestered for their opinions.

Acknowledgments

Cover photograph: Edinburgh Castle and the Old Town seen from Arthur's Seat; Jonathan Smith/Getty Images.

This Book

This 3rd edition of Lonely Planet's *Pocket Edinburgh* guidebook was researched and written by Neil Wilson. The previous two editions were also written by Neil Wilson. This guidebook was commissioned in Lonely Planet's London office, and produced by the following:

Commissioning Editor Clifton Wilkinson **Coordinating Editors** Carolyn Bain, Kate James **Senior Cartographer** Jennifer Johnston **Coordinating Layout Designer** Lauren Egan **Managing Editor** Angela Tinson **Senior Editor** Catherine Naghten **Managing Layout Designer** Chris Girdler

Assisting Cartographer Rachel Imeson **Cover Research** Naomi Parker **Internal Image Research** Kylie McLaughlin **Thanks to** Anita Banh, Ryan Evans, Larissa Frost, Genesys India, Jouve India, Wayne Murphy, Trent Paton, Kerrianne Southway, Gerard Walker

Index

See also separate subindexes for:

⊗ **Eating p166**

⊕ **Drinking p167**

✪ **Entertainment p167**

⊙ **Shopping p167**

Sights p000
Map Pages **p000**

Our Writer

Neil Wilson

Neil was born in Glasgow but defected to the east at the age of 18 and has now lived in Edinburgh for more than 30 years. While studying at Edinburgh University he spent long, lazy summer afternoons exploring the closes, wynds, courtyards and backstreets of his adopted city; since then, he has continued to delve into Edinburgh's many hidden corners, taking a special interest in the city's pubs and restaurants. Neil has been a full-time writer and photographer since 1988 and has written more than 50 guidebooks for various publishers, including the Lonely Planet guide to Scotland.

Published by Lonely Planet Publications Pty Ltd
ABN 36 005 607 983
3rd edition – January 2014
ISBN 978 1 74220 049 1
© Lonely Planet 2014 Photographs © as indicated 2014
10 9 8 7 6 5 4 3
Printed in China